Cocaine Poems Part I
Poet

Leon J. Gratton

Grosvenor House
Publishing Limited

All rights reserved
Copyright © Leon J. Gratton, 2024

The right of Leon J. Gratton to be identified as the author of this
work has been asserted in accordance with Section 78
of the Copyright, Designs and Patents Act 1988

The book cover is copyright to Leon J. Gratton

This book is published by
Grosvenor House Publishing Ltd
Link House
140 The Broadway, Tolworth, Surrey, KT6 7HT.
www.grosvenorhousepublishing.co.uk

This book is sold subject to the conditions that it shall not, by way of
trade or otherwise, be lent, resold, hired out or otherwise circulated
without the author's or publisher's prior consent in any form of
binding or cover other than that in which it is published and
without a similar condition including this condition being
imposed on the subsequent purchaser.

This book is a work of fiction. Any resemblance to
people or events, past or present, is purely coincidental.

A CIP record for this book
is available from the British Library

ISBN 978-1-80381-934-1

November Tenth

Liam was on the inter-city 125 from Lincoln to Edinburgh he had made a large purchase of party powder (cocaine) and was already lining up customers. He smiled at his auntie who was just as sly as she was old. And they had buried the cocaine in five jars of coffee. An ounce ball in each. They weren't expecting company in the way of polis but they had to be careful. As you never know who could be selling you out. The train arrived in the station and Liam's auntie told him to get back to his flat in Calder's. He smiled as she waved at him as her taxi drove her back to her home in Calder's. His first port of call was his regular drinking place Misfits. He walked in and gave a nod to the barman and a nod to the local bouncer.

He walked over to Shimmey, who was in his usual spot, just of the bar in a quiet wee corner. Pinkie saw Liam heading over to them and stood up and they gripped wrists.

"Did Grandad do his time?" Asked Liam. who had been down in Lincoln making the cocaine connection.

Pinkie smiled and said. "You know the score, dinnea dae the crime if you cannea dae the time".

Liam nodded at this statement. "And you Shimmey are testament to that fact," continued Liam.

Shimmey nodded and bit the wick off a newly rolled spliff. Then blazed it up with a brass zippo. Then he said, "Aye I did my stint. Seven months".

Liam sniffed in and took the joint fae Shimmey. Shimmey continued his spiel, "Aye, anyway they still cannea pin the fucking robbery on us."

The pub began to fill slowly with regulars and passing trade. They sat with a jug of Tennent's lager each. And they had a blaze as-well. They sat and roached at least five joints. And the night was still young, Pinkie smiled, "Did yea score doon there?" He asked.

"Aye it's gonna be a white Christmas," came the reply of Liam.

"Aye how much did you score and what kind?"

Liam smiled, "Top quality uncut Bolivian gold flake".

Pinkie laughed. "Aye sound as a pound", he said as they carried on drinking and toking.

"What's this I heard you, were in hiding down in Manchester?"

Pinkie's eyes glinted like this was the only time he got mischievous. When he was blagging and bragging. "No, it was fun and games for like two months".

Liam asked the question that was dying to be asked. "What's this Paul Kelly like?" Pinkie smiled and replied, "Chill as fuck super fucking cool".

*

They went their separate ways and headed to their homes and dens, Pinkie his den in Sighthill and Shimmey walked home to the top of Wester Hailes Park. Grandad was due to be released a fortnight after the Bells.

And then he would be kicking motherfucking ass. He was not happy at how sloppy things had gotten since his incarceration. It was as if they had gotten fat and lazy and decided to just, well, just no bother, they were well they were becoming really stupid and lazy. As if reaching the crown and top of the Young Casual game and it would be theirs forever, but this wasn't so. No the skulls were on the rise and were posing a great threat to the YBC, but the YBC had just dismissed it as if they were a minor team.

But Grandad knew different. He had ears, he kept the pulse and general word of the street in his sights. But being dubbed up was not helping things and he only had a minor control over things, Liam had kept as much contact with Grandad as he could and Grandad told him with exactly what to do, keep all the pipelines for narcotics open and keep them running smooth. Liam did as he was told. It was Grandad that had sent him the details of the cocaine buy. Grandad rested his head, listening to some Neil Young and the Crazy Horse. The album *Harvest*.

Dawn had long since vanished from the life of Grandad, it was upsetting but totally unavoidable. Grandad had just over six weeks to go. And he sure as hell wasn't going to fight or get pushed into a corner where he had to defend himself. Most people saw him as a peaceful calming quiet soldier. Who was only interested in doing his time neatly and quietly. He had no cellmate so no problem with territory. Only a few of the other inmates had a bug up their asses, but it had got sorted without bloodshed. No, their bosses and friends kept them back, out of respect, especially after the Leeds massacres. They had done the deed that needed to be done. But still the rat remained a problem.

He kept one eye on the gate of prison (watching who was coming and going). The other eye on his patch; Sighthill and Broomie. Biscuit was talking about hanging his spurs up and still Leeds couldn't respond with another attack. Grandad just had to pray nothing happened whilst he was inside Polmont. He would just have to keep his heed doon and get on with the time he had been given.

*

Liam got to his flat in Calder and rushed straight to the stash place where his auntie would have left the five cocaine balls. He was going to weigh and bag as much as he could. He opened up the stash in the floorboards next to the living room window. There they were but he was one short, his Auntie must be doing some punting of her own, that didn't surprise him, no it didn't surprise him at all, he laughed, fuck crossing her she was as cunning as the most notorious of gangsters and boy did he know it.

He began to chop and weigh the product in grammes. With an electric set of scales that measured point two of a gramme and up. These were really useful as he may need to weigh some smack. And the scales never lie. This was a big thing on the streets.

"The scales never lie," He said as carried on bagging the coke. He finished a little after four in the morning, and decided to write in his diary, which was mental notes and Poems, most of the poems were about Gemma and the code of the streets. He did not preach to anyone, nor did he force his poetry on anyone. As he found that in life as well as in death there is a certain poetic justice. Pertaining to us all.

November Eleventh

Liam woke to the thumping of the door.
"Alright, alright, I'm coming, I'm coming," he said. There at his door was his old mucker Biscuit.

Biscuit smiled at him, "How yea daen Liam?" They immediately embraced. "Been a while huh?" said Biscuit.

"Yeah Man too long," Replied Liam. Biscuit took a swig of the Miller's beer he was holding and said, "Well can I come in?"

Liam smiled and stepped aside. "You need any white?" Liam said as they walked to the Living room, "Yeah Man, is it speed?" Liam smiled and replied, "No man, its cocaine".

Biscuit looked around at the ramshackled flat and said, "Then definitely.

Liam produced a gramme in a bag and said, "On the house".

Biscuit smiled and said, "Much appreciated".

Liam smiled, it had been nearly a year since they had met last. And that was during the period when he was put in hospital. He smiled and Biscuit asked him, if he had a bubble.

Liam said, "fuck yeah, I'll just go and get it".

He then went into the kitchen and fished out his small crack pipe. He then produced a regal, lit the thing and tipped the ash on the gauze and dropped a pinch of cocaine onto it. He handed the bubble to Liam, who immediately lit the coke and toked the creamy vanilla smoke. He smiled and then sat down, as he handed the pipe back to Liam. Liam took a smoke and enjoyed his eleven o'clock morning rush. They spraffed for a while then Biscuit, feeling as though he had made up time with Liam smiled and walked back home.

He was technically on annual leave from Beatties building firm, but knew he would have to go back to work some time. It wasn't as if the drug world had any hold over him and after they failed in the executing of the contract on Biscuit he was nearly through with that whole life. He was confident that he could live life without drugs (that meaning only recreational drugs, you know, a weekender). He was just wanting to see if Grandad had really made it big. This would satisfy his curiosity into who held him the most, was it Pinkie, Gizmo, Shimmey or Liam.

He figured on it being Liam. As the two of them had spent a long and uncontrollable period of a state of Munted. They were inseparable. Liam would tell Biscuit that he had never met anyone quite like him and that it was an honour to get stoned with him. Biscuit smiled when he said this and the two of them got more stoned, and Liam became a firm favourite of his. They went to pubs up on the Bridges and pubs on Rose Street. Liam would bring Gemma and Biscuit would bring Suzzane. The two of them stepped out like this every month or so.

*

Pinkie woke up to the sound of the Bin Lorry emptying the Bins in the bin Chutes. They finished and Pinkie rolled over and got himself a fag, he lit up and smoked his lungs back to working order. Then it was, yep you guessed it, a bottle of Grolsch. He swigged the thing thinking, 'Life could be a hell of a lot worse'. Pinkie switched on the radio, Absolute Classic Rock. The song, *Wanted Dead or Alive* by Bon Jovi. He felt a kinship to this song but then so did half of Edinburgh. He smiled as the song came to an end, he knew who he was visiting that afternoon and that was Liam.

Pinkie smiled as he crossed the distance to Liam's. He got to the stairwell and buzzed the intercom.

"Hello?" Came the question from Liam.

"Aye it's me Pinkie," He said.

"Come up", was returned by Liam. Pinkie could feel a healthy session coming, he had a fair-sized lump of dope on him, and knew that it would be needed for the come down. He smiled as he reached Liam's door. Liam stood there stretching as Pinkie reached the doorway.

"Awright Pinkie?" Came the question from Liam.

Pinkie answered, "Aye man you got the white?" Liam smiled and said, "Aye man come in".

They headed straight to the living room and Pinkie was feeling the buzz before it even started. He sat down and was handed the bubble with enough ash and enough cocaine to send him into a nice state of ecstasy. He then produced fifty pounds for a fair size piece of crack. Liam handed him the baggie then put the money into his pocket. Pinkie immediately reloaded the bubble and whoosh the rush hit him as he lit up the small pipe.

They began to get nice and wasted. Shimmey and Giz were next at his door as the two of them were curious to see how much he had. Liam let them in and Giz was carrying a bag full of Becks beer. At least twelve bottles.

Pinkie rolled a joint and passed the bubble clockwise. They were in a state of utter bliss. The cocaine was doing exactly what it was supposed to do. All they needed was the hooches, you know, the birds. And that could be sorted with a quick phone call. Giz went down to the local phone box and called Hazel and her best friends.

"Aye Hazel we got a great score, want to come and help us polish it off?"

Haze smiled, she was a pretty lass with brown hair and gentle features "Can I bring a couple of friends?"

Giz smiled down the phone, "Aye doll the more the merrier. She giggled a little and replied, "I'll be there in two hours".

Giz chuckled, "Aye and bring Cargo with you".

She smiled and started to get ready for a day of crack cocaine, she called Lisa Aldershaw, then she called Angela Noble and Suzzane Gaffney, and they made the journey from Carricknowe to Calders. They were let in instantly. And handed over the money for a gramme each. Hazel straight away began to rack up the lines for them to snort. The mirror from the Bathroom was brought through to the living room and the powder was plentiful. The music went on and it was Jamiroqua (Acid Jazz).

*

Meanwhile the Skulls were having a sit down, a war meeting with Boz as the head of affairs. He was sick and tired of being second best in an area which he should run. He was planning on seeing to the YBC. But this was easier said than done, he and his crew had never been beaten and the only team that showed any kind of resistance was the YBC, especially after the war with

Leeds. But Boz was adamant in the fact he was going to run West Edinburgh and no one was going to stop him and the WHSC. He smiled and spoke to his right-hand man, Mikey. Now, Mikey was a handsome lad who showed no fear. And often as not he had gotten bloody and had never received a scratch. Boz on the other hand had been in lots of ruck's and had been on the receiving end of a good fight. But that was the thing about Boz he had the courage and skill to run his Manor, the rest of the skulls looked up to Boz they knew he was game. And the more trouble you sent at him the more Psychotic and blood thirsty he got. He was a mad acid head and was tripping constantly. He never had a bad trip and always gleamed of the acid.

The meeting was called and they began to discuss the action that they needed to bring in to the game, but some of the heads were worried and it showed in their lack of trust. Some of them believed the whole war was a waste of time and they should seek another less violent way, a truce. Boz threw a flaky fit soon as this was raised.

"We've been courteous," He said then growled.

Mikey was turning a roach in his hand and gave the joint to Boz. Boz smiled at him and said, "Thanks Mikey". Then carried on scolding the rest of them.

"We cannea let them see weakness. Coz they will do everything to exploit that," Boz took a toke from his joint. "Any way we are too far down the road to let things settle, and I have plans, big plans for this side of toon".

Mikey smiled at the rest of the war council. "you will do well to remember that it's us that got you this far". He said.

They then all broke out with drugs and finished with a high instead of wasting the day with a lot of Bullshit.

The night sailed on with Beastie boys *Sabotage* playing in the background. 'Ahh can't stand it, I know you planned it'. They song brought a smile to Boz's face he knew well the dangers of paranoia.

*

Grandad sat in his cell smoking a fag and listening to Pink Floyd, the album was *Animals*. 'And watching for pigs on the wing' swam through the hall. He smiled thinking that things were going to be sweet when he was released. He was looking forward to a cold bottle of beer and a nice joint of soft black gold seal. He sat back and carried on listening to Pink Floyd.

Grandad had been a model prisoner from day one and the Guv'nor respected that. He had called a halt to the war that was happening on his doorstep. He knew he had the troops and that most of the other gangs had backed off. But things were too quiet with the hood. His cousin had sent him a couple of letters, telling him how the streets had calmed down after he was arrested. This sat well with Gramps, and Grandad knew that he was well respected. He had made a small pact with a couple of the other inmates and that had made him a powerful inmate.

He had done his time quietly and had been well rewarded from the Guv'nor of the YO. He had been privileged from day one. He even managed to score a couple bags of kit and the YO wasn't too bad in the needle exchange side of things. So he managed to shoot up now and then. But this was only occasionally and he had to tread water with the cold turkey side of things. But he counted his blessings and got his heed doon.

November Thirteenth

The fucking party turned into an orgy. And they all got good and wet. The thing lasted two days and punters came and went giving Liam a nice bit of change in his pocket. A couple of the local lads made an appearance and scored. And he didn't give out that much tick. But he made a huge dent in the cocaine that he had. Kingo was one of his regulars and had made a large purchase of about seven gramme and paid for it up front. Liam was pleased with this. That gave him a good overhead of money. Pinkie smiled whilst taking a toke of a bubble whilst getting his cock sucked by Angie Noble. It was heaven. The music carried on it was Bonkers, the rave set by Tiny Tempa. They had waited all year for this score, and Liam had delivered. Christmas was going to be great, or so they thought.

*

Boz sat back in his armchair smiling as the thought of destroying the YBC. He had just shot up and it was clean and decent. No the War was unavoidable and he relished that thought. It was open season on Broom Toon and he was going to play a major part in their fall. He called on his staffie. "Boscoe," he shouted and the dog came running into the sitting room and Boz gave him a treat. A doggie chocolate biscuit. The dog sat on the couch whilst Boz skinned up and started to play some music. And that music was Pink Floyd's *The Wall*. He went to his stash and made sure it was all there. He had Walls, he had Jaggers, he had Microdots; red, black and green. He also had a shit load of speed, he was just waiting to make deliveries. Two more days and him and Boscoe would be heading for the various dealers and pushers. He looked at his book collection, where he had a lot by various gangs from around the world. He had *Arrivederci Millwall*, *Bloody Casuals* (Aberdeen) and *Hibs boy* (CCS). He took pride in what he read and also he had the Kray Twins. There were a number of books about them. Their kindness and charity to runaway kids made them legendary. It was just this kind of heart that made you wonder if the other side were the worse of the two. You know ACAB, God knows they proved their name as bastards to the underworld. And sometimes innocent people were caught in the firing line. You know caught with a small amount of drugs. But the police had no conscience. They were often heavy handed. And well you didn't want to make one of them an enemy, they were partial to using mace. Boz wasn't worried about them, he could handle the scrapping and he had become proficient in their ways. And knew how to deal with them, but the thing that remained a truly deep secret was how deep were Boz's pockets. Who was he in bed with. Mikey knocked on the door of Boz's flat.

"Who is it?" Came Boz's voice whilst Boscoe barked as the door was rapped again.

"It's me, Mikey," Came the reply.

Boz laughed and opened the door. "Took your time," He said and gripped the top of the doorway then moved aside to let Mikey in. He passed the joint he had just rolled and lit. Mikey smiled and said, "You want me to take yer dug oot?"

Boz laughed, "Aye and make sure he does both before you bring him back".

Mikey slipped the choker leash over the lethal wee fuckers neck. "Come on Boscoe," He said and gave a shrill whistle. They were gone twenty minutes.

Boz started to count out the money that had just been paid to him from various tick lists. He smiled and laughed and said as Mikey returned.

"It's all there," Boz sighed and said, "Too mad. It's been a long time since we panned oot".

Mikey re lit the doobie and said, "Aye well it was messy".

Boz clapped his dug and said, "How messy? Couple of slaps and a couple of breaks," replied Mikey.

"I hope you wurnea to soft on them?" said Boz as he carried on petting his Staffie.

"Nah man, I was as cool as I could be, considering," replied Mikey. Boz carried on petting as he puffed on a joint. Mikey stayed around for a while.

*

Pinkie finished his gramme in superb style, a line and a pull on the bubble. Then he went and got himself a beer to quench the thirst that he had, Then after the beer he went back to his den down in Sighthill. He hadn't the stomach for another gramme. He racked his brain trying to figure out how much he had tanned in the last two days. It was a minor matter and didn't concern him too much. The smile and shine on him was too good to be true, happy days.

He got himself another beer. He figured it out about two gramme, that was it two gramme he had tanned. He was well wary of the time and knew that it would only be a couple of weeks until Grandad was released. And then a party, a huge, massive, glad to be alive party for Gramps, and he would be main man again, the profits of the Manchester connection were flowing and had tripled in the last three months. Grandad still thought they were getting sloppy. No hunger and no desire. But that would change as soon as he got released. He would kick ass and made sure that they hadn't gotten to soft. It was, well, a tough break and nothing was surer than the fact that they were still on the edge of war. And Grandad knew exactly who it was.

The Skulls. Grandad and the YBC had three hundred soldiers and he was counting on them being ready when he got released, Cha and Raymie were keeping the narcotics under scrutiny, And doing a fine job of it to. They had made the run to Manchester three four times and never even got pulled by the Bizzies. Cha was a cool coper when it came to the product. The Angel hair itself was popular. And also the Northen Lights Grass. They were also in possession of three thousand eckies of various sorts. Including Hearts and Mitsubishis and Fioris. And some would say the cream was a potent little ecstasy tablet scooby snacks. They were running a clean little business into the heart of the rave culture, and it was coming up trumps.

Cha spoke to Grandad on the phone. "Aye Gramps, the product is still quality".

Grandad smiled at this as he was still unsure of the numbers. "Are we still making the connection in the Mancunian connection?" Asked Gramps.

Cha smiled his wee pearlies out. "Aye it's all good Grandad, I've been overseeing the transactions myself, everything is kosher".

Grandad nodded his head and produced a fag. "Paul still sound?" Cha snorted and replied, "Aye man that guy is so chill that he would never be caught even if he was caught, you catch my drift".

Grandad blew a couple of doughnuts of his fag. "Yeah well it's coming up my release date, and I don't want to rely on hopes and dreams, this is my greatest concern".

They finished talking and Grandad hung up the phone. He was thinking everything is good. And that he wouldn't have to get bloody as it appeared that Cha and Raymie were in control of the situation. But something was bugging Grandad and he hoped it wasn't who he thought it was and that was the skulls.

November Twentieth

Liam was cutting some nice coke and mixing it with angel hair. To make what it was known as a Chinese Bomb. He had to meet someone from a recording studio down in London. She was a gorgeous blond hippy chick called Kate. And Liam was totally fixated with her as she was a total trip to be around. He met her at the Elephant coffee shop on the Bridges where he would be assured a good price for an ounce of chopped Chinese Bombs. He was hoping to score a big score, he sat down across from her and felt good about the drop. She smiled and he smiled back. She was a beauty in a down dressed Amanda de Cadenet kind of way. She was a total screw and Liam knew it.

She smiled and said, "You want a cappuccino Liam?"

Liam smiled and responded, "aye doll". #She caught the waitress and said, "two cappuccinos please".

The waitress smiled and said, "Coming right up".

Liam smiled as the frothy, milky coffee was brought to their table. The hot chocolate on top was enough sweetness for Liam. She smiled as they sipped their coffees, Liam pushed a small baggie with the product in it enough to give her a decent hit. She then proceeded to go to the bathroom to have a quick line. She came back and sat down. The smile shone in her eyes and now she was high.

COCAINE POEMS PART 1: POET

"Good enough?" Came the question from Liam.

She smiled sweetly and said, "How much?"

Liam smiled even more. "I'll take seven hundred for the ounce".

She smiled back at him. "That's a deal matey".

He knew that he could get more for it if he sold it gramme for gramme. But he really didn't want to lose this connection. In the background was the gorillas song 'I got sunshine in a bag',

They finished their coffees then went to Kate's house. They got to the stairwell and she dropped to her knees and began to squeeze the bulge in his pants. He smiled as his thick cock sprung out his trousers. She began to gobble the juicy fat cock of Liam and Liam began to count his blessings.

"God save the Queen, God save Rangers." He was about to say God save the Pope but no, he ejaculated all over her face. They then went up the stairs to her flat and made love. Just as he was about leave she paid him with three one hundred pound notes and the rest in twenties. He smiled and wandered back to his flat in Calder's.

He was waiting back at his flat he knew this was a bit self-indulgent but knew he had to share the wealth. Shimmey and pinkie arrived on his doorstep half an hour after he came back home. Liam smiled and handed them a hundred pound note each and kept one for himself. These would be used in the snorting of cocaine. Liam was In his element. He began to tell the tale of the blow job he had just received.

*

Biscuit was having a nice cool joint, letting the smoke go deep into his lungs. All the while he was thinking, thank god I'm me. Suzzane entered and walked through to the sitting room.

"You okay sweetness?" She asked as she sat down.

"Aye doll" He replied then continued, "Liams back".

She smiled at him and nodded her head. "I take it you'll be wanting to go oot on the toon?" Biscuit smiled and handed her the joint "He's got really, really good white".

She looked at her man, wondering whether he would ever be brave enough to propose to her. Probably not, was the answer she had come up with and she had asked herself that question a few times. She even felt compelled to propose to him, she thought about it and knew that it was a while away until the next leap year. And tradition dictated that it only was on a leap year that a woman could propose to her man. And you know how shy women are at the best of times. Never finding the actual guts to make plans to grab a man's attention and hold them steadfast.

Then say, "Will you marry me?".

It came in at an old fashioned will you got to bed with me scenario. And women were lousy at seduction at the best of times. They were shy and stupid. And weren't brave enough to take the matter in hand. No it was a nightmare situation just trying to hold the relationship together, never mind the thought of commitment. She sighed and handed him back the joint. He smiled winked at her and she fell in love with him all over again. This happened on a weekly basis. She would confuse herself with over blown feelings and think a long way down the road. Always for nought she could go insane thinking and feeling this way. But she held on she held on tight.

*

Liam walked over to his aunt's house to see if things were faring well with her. He knocked on the door. Liam smiled a goofy stoned smile that will never fade. Anyone gazing at him would assume he was well, well stoned. And it took years to build up a habit like his. A non-relenting non plussed way that was only coming from years of hanging about the streets. He liked being wasted, it gave him a final sense of appeasement. He smiled and fixed his hair then knocked on the door and entered his aunt's house.

She was in the kitchen cooking up a storm. She was making carbonara a favourite of his and he would stay for dinner. She smiled as she served up the dish to him. The cream, the egg, the bacon, the spaghetti and the cheese. He was overwhelmed with the scent of the beautiful cream cheese and parmesan cheese. He tucked into the meal that was fit for a king, he had a profound respect for his aunt, and she did for him.

"Okay Aunt Marion." He said, "What's for pudding?"

She smiled and said, "Your favourite, baked rice." He smiled and said, "Bring it on Aunt Marion bring it on."

She went and got the casserole dish with the rice and raisins and vanilla and grated on top was nutmeg. He finished his meal then spoke to her.

"You get a good price for that party powder?"

Marion rolled her eyes back into her skull. "Yeah, yeah, it was a nice bit of flake son".

He smiled and pulled out a little vial and spoon and fixed his beak. He then opened a tin of Budweiser. He smiled and sat back and started to watch the telly with his aunt who was watching Mobsters. The film about 'Lucky Luciano' and the beginning of their rise to infamy. It was a good part for Christian Slater and he played the part well. He stayed and watched the film then after it finished he headed into town to Gemma's house just off the West End of Edinburgh's Princes Street.

He stood before her door and rapped on the heavy piece of wood. She came dressed as if she had just stepped out of the shower, her hair was wet and tied up in a towel. She looked at him and said, "Honey pie your back".

Liam stood there and said, "Aye doll, aye I'm hame".

She ushered him into the grandiose house and straight into her bedroom. He pulled out a small bag of cocaine. He only had a couple of ounces left But, it would stretch for another couple of weeks. All things being relative and nothing happening that couldn't be set right with a bribe or a fight. He had often dusted of his knuckles with a square go for money and he was a brilliant and undefeated boxer.

Not just some knuckle head trying to make a name for himself. And there were plenty of fights on the go. And he had got the reputation as a hard man. But a just man as well. He never parted company on a bitter note and always tried to keep himself in check. If something was wrong instead of blowing a gasket, he would pull himself together and try to reason things out. Violence was a last resort. But if it got too much, he would lose his cool as something was always popping off. And his temper was constantly being tested. He smiled as he went into Gemma's bedroom, she took off her clothes and began to crawl on him.

He smiled as her dark hair spilled onto his chest and he felt her vibrant body tremble on his legs and stomach as they began to kiss. They necked and spooned for a good half an hour. The time they had spent apart from each other, and now they would need to make up for lost time. Liam was happily intrigued with his lover's ways in the bedroom. She was a special kind of lover an exquisite and only his type of lover. She had never made a noise in the way of their love. She was content and he was more than a good lover, no he was tender and soft. And took his time enjoying both giving and receiving the sexual stimuli. They were always experiencing new and wonderful ways in the days of drugs sex and rock and roll. Liam was accounted as a well of and much praised man of the hour. He hadn't come easily of that title. And took its meaning seriously. It was right up there with Top Boy.

*

Cha and Raymie were languidly lounging in boredom at the recent turn of events. They had done the month's mule run down to Manchester and now they had little else to do but get munted. They were playing cards waiting for the phone to ring with the accounts of said drug run. They were waiting to hear how much profit they had made. It tripled last month with the angel hair smack being as popular as ever so they had to cut it twice. But this had left them short for the following month. But Cha and Raymie bartered a good deal with

Paul and left with a sizable lump of Tarrie. A nice piece of soft black Moroccan. It was one of those rare types of dope that was highly sought after. And everybody knew that Paul was the man to see about rare pieces of dope. This left him with very little time to spend on himself, but the money was good ('cause if it wasn't he would tell the chiefs to stick it).

Paul smiled as he extinguished the match he had lit the joint up with, he did so with a little flick. Grandad on the other hand would light a match with his thumb nail. This was a good party trick. And there were lots of said tricks especially with matches, the other thing that was good was a zippo lighter. Grandad could light a zippo with the snap of his finger. They also light one on their jeans. Flicking the hood of the Zippo then lighting it as quick as they could. Paul smiled, he missed Scotty, they all did and knew that he was locked up, so said a prayer for him. But he was getting out soon and Paul knew they would have some catching up to do. The whole Manchester connection had been Grandad's doing. But this just left the thought who was the rat. Paul had suspicions on who it was, but they had been clever keeping their name out of courtroom documents. But still they had been played, and Paul wasn't going to rest until he found the dirty cheese eating prick. A couple of times when he was just starting out as a cannabis dealer he had a boy make rather large purchases, Paul had mentioned this to Grandad who looked the boy up and down with a Sicilian scowl.

Paul said, "That boy just made a large purchase".

Grandad continued to look at the guy and replied, "He looks out of place",

Paul sniffed in and carried on talking, "Couple of ounce he just purchased".

Grandad continued to look the boy over. "He want a street discount I take it?"

Paul scoffed, "Yeah he did, the balls on the guy huh?"

Grandad motioned for Polland to come over then whispered in Polland's ear "Follow that fuck, Paul's a bit suspicious of the guy?"

Polland watched and waited for the guy to leave then carefully stalked him. That night was burned into Grandad's and Paul's heads. Two weeks later, when Grandad had returned to Scotland, Paul was busted and charge with the selling and distribution of a controlled substance. He blew the charge out his arse of course. And the guy who Polland followed to his house in Bury, well they never saw him again. A bit too much of a coincidence. Grandad vowed, if he ever saw the guy again he would tan him. Paul sent Grandad a gift to his jail, it was the double album *The Wall* by Pink Floyd. Grandad got the tape and sent a quick note saying thanks. The usual happened when sending mail to and from jail, it was opened and searched for drugs and Illicit content. But still the double album *The Wall*. He played it every day. This got on the other Inmates tits, but still he played it sometimes twice a day.

November Twenty-seventh

Liam was climbing the walls with the hangover. He and the rest of his crew were adamant that they weren't going to stop partying until Grandad was released. And that day they would party even more. Grandad got his heed doon and carried on his sentence. The days were crawling in boredom. And his habit was only partially satiated. He had a classic come down symptoms and he knew he had to hold on until he scored another bag of heroin.

He smiled and smoked his baccy. It was a luxury that he had a single cell to himself and that Shimmey and Giz had got out just before each of their sentencing had come to an end. They had got out a few days early. And straight into the arms of the YBC. They smiled as their friends and families opened their arms and showered them in dope and beer. Grandad was jealous but there was nothing he could do about it. Grandad smiled as he remembered the location of the money that the polis were trying to find.

Clever no, Grandad was a genius when it came to loot. He would send a large portion of it up north and into a Fish Yard where he would begin to smuggle in drugs from across the water. Amsterdam and other

Scandinavian countries that had large chemical factories. The money for the Kilsyth Robbery, well it was tied up in cocaine and heroin, as well as ecstasy and other drugs Like LSD and Northern Lights grass. Nobody knew his connections nobody other than the connections themselves. They didn't have to keep track as it all did it by itself. The bank account he used, well, his Uncle kept tabs on it. And he watched it swell by itself. The money was deposited before the product was delivered. This was so and it was all paid for in advance. The Kilsyth Heist had set them up double what they needed. And profits well profits were good.

Dawn had been in contact a couple of times but the relationship had run its course and she had moved on, she explained it to him and he took it like a man. She was in love with a surfer dude who had the charm and wit of Californian man.

She left him saying, "You know how it is Leon, people move on".

Grandad sat back in his billet and said, "Yeah I know how it is".

The pain was insufferable, so he cooked up a jail house shot and spiked his vein and stopped the pain. His mam was about to visit him. She had various things like chocolate and baccy. These were a luxury and he knew it. She had driven the width of Scotland to make sure he was at least a semblance of himself, he looked pained and gaunt. And his habit was tearing him up as-well as Dawn dumping him.

"After what you did for her, she dumps you?"

Grandad smiled and itched his left arm, he was coming down "The lassie didnea fit in wae me and my crew anyway takes a load of, of my back as she was a target for the other Crews anyhow".

His mam reached over to molly coddle him, he backed away.

"Mam," he said as she carried on trying to feel if he had a fever. "Mam, dinea".

She stopped and said, "I should give her a piece of my mind".

Grandad sighed and said as she left, "Brilliant that's all I need my mam on the warpath".

*

Liam carried on Snorting the coke with his mint, green note. With one hundred on it. Shimmey and Pinkie were doing the same with their notes. They smiled 'cat has got the cream' smiles, as they tore through an ounce of cocaine. Liam got up after the nose powder and said, "I got to phone and score, you know more, more, more".

The three of them smiled and carried on. Liam went down the stairs to the local phone box and dialled his connection.

"Alright Shazza," he said then began to buzz oot o his nut, asking if she was able to hook up with him and bring some product. She smiled and replied, "Yes Liam, I got what you need".

He smiled and waited for her to make the dates and times.

"Two days and how much you wanting?"

He smiled feeling the excitement growing in him, "Five ounce again please Shazza and that should last me well into the New Year". He smiled and continued.

"Same price for same gear?" He asked, she smiled and said, "Yeah man, that'll be top".

"Okay I'll see you in two days Edinburgh Waverley".

"Yes hun yes". She finished and he hung up. He went back up to his flat. When he arrived back Pinkie had just loaded a bubble for the three of them. He sat down and took a long puff of the crack pipe. Then began to rush, he smiled feeling the warm smoke visit his lungs.

"So we on for more product?" Asked Shimmey.

Liam smiled and shook his head, "Two more days and we'll be back in business".

Pinkie smiled and snorted another line. "Good man Liam". He said then sniffed the fine white powder right down his nasal cavity and began to rush on the powder. Smiling he lit up a fag and relaxed on the sofa.

"Anyway I got other plans," he said and began to look through the book that was left lying around *'The Lords and the New creatures'* He couldn't believe how a book of poetry could hold anyone's attention. But this one did it was about the cinema and JFK. How messy society was then. Then the unrequited love poem at the end, knowing you had no hope with the hippie love chick as she was in love with the Iron Horseman (Hell's Angel). He got up and put on the CD *Morrison Hotel*. Roadhouse Blues was the first track on the CD then it travelled all the way to Blue Sunday.

"I love you the Best, Better than all the rest". The music set the night right up. And it was followed by the rest of the Doors albums. They then sent Shimmey down to get some beers. He smiled and put his hand in his pocket and decided for once he couldn't be stingy. No he had a veritable duty to buy him and his two compadres beers. He smiled and went and bought a crate of Miller bottles of beer. Twenty-four in total. He smiled as he got back into the house and began to off-load the cargo into the giant fridge and took three out of the pack and they started to hau a swallie. Things were roses. Giz showed up at the door after about ten minutes of the cargo being drank.

"Awright Giz?" said Liam.

Giz shook his head and replied, "Yeah man. I could use a line bring me back to life. Liam smiled and ushered him into the sitting room where he proceeded to have a pull on the Crack bubble. Liam smiled as the smoke was exhaled by Gizmo. He handed him a miller cold one. They sat and passed the bubble and lined up lines of coke on a mirror with a sticker that said Bite my Bum then there was a cheeky little angel pointing it's bum at you. It got a lot of action Gemma had put it there. The mirror was pristine and had been well used.

They began to talk about the good old days with grandad. And the rest of the YBC. They had many tales to tell, fights and so forth. Giz was telling the one about the chippy and the three boys Grandad and Nichol and Ali Grey Giz and James. These two boy's had been giving Grandad the eyeball on their way home from WHEC. The local school for what Leon called 'Wester Aliens' They were game enough but Grandad didn't back down. He charged the two of them. Took a few and dished a few. Then they left, but this wusnea over fir Gramps, no he wanted to hunt them doon. And he had done so that summer. One of them was walking their dog by the Flats and Grandad who was tripping with Baby Muz. They ran at the boy and his ane dug bit him as he got the fear. Leon threw a trolley, a supermarket trolley, at him. Grandad had a good seven eight hours of the two trips he had taken. Any way the two of them were at the chippy just down fae the silver wing and they had a friend who was disputed to be a broomie boy his name was Medi.

Grandad walked right up to them and punched the little shit on the nose. The other two dropped their chips and tried to run but Nichol launched at one of them Jumping and punching the shithead on the back of his heed. Grandad began to set about the two of them whilst Ali Grey smashed one as-well. They ran home to their mammies and Grandad's honour was satisfied.

*

Biscuit wet his beak again with some more party powder. He had scored a couple of gramme rocks off of Liam. He cut the drugs with Bicarbonate of Soda and Suzzanne was in the middle of rolling a spliff with some nice slate. It was dry and rough but nice and sweet at the same time. And there was a load of it on the street. Nobody had been busted in ages and nobody had been a cowboy either. No, things were at a state of grace with the law giving a knife armistice and people who wanted peace handed in their stashes of blades, it was a good thing too, it cut the knife crime in two. Which, if you ask me was fine so far. And the Paranoia eased a little on the streets, people were more accepting of cannabis and speed.

More people had more tolerance and people were high for high's sake. They even moved the class B drug, Cannabis, into the class C category. Which was one more reason for the dope trend. It was looking hopeful. We saw the wisdom of the streets and that was why we hung about so long enjoying ourselves. Things couldn't be much better. Biscuit carried on rocking back and drinking and smoking. On his Hi-fi that was blasting was the song 'Skills to pay the Bills, What bills?' The Beastie Boys. He smiled as Suzzane sat down on his lap and whispered into his ear. "Next time they are in Scotland, we'll go and see them".

He smiled and took a kiss of her in agreement. They sat and listened to the Beastie Boys all night then when the dope ran dry they went to bed and made sweet love.

November Thirtieth

Boz was finishing off the drug run he and Mikey had been hoping too, as quickly as possible. They were at the last dealers door and waited for him to answer. He wasn't a problematic dealer, he just used a little too much ecstasy. And it reflected on his sales. But Boz was patient and had enough time to gather the monies from the local population. It was just this guy, Norman Rockwell, he had too many excuses.

"If you fuck up one more time," said Boz as he laid the product down on the kitchen table, "I will swing for you and unlike your punters, I won't miss".

Norman smiled, "Then what?" came from Norman.

"You'll be deed," said Mikey who produced his Microtek Halo. A wicked razor-sharp flick knife that the special forces carried. It was gleaming as he held it there in front of Normans face.

"Okay, okay I'll pay on time," Norman responded.

"Whatever you dae Norman, remember I'm number one roond here".

Norman smiled an uneasy smile and replied. "You'll no get any problems with me, I swear Boz, I'll make sure they all pay".

He laughed at the cowardice of the dealer then Mikey and himself left.

"No ambition," Mikey laughed and turned on the ignition to his Ford Capri. It was a bit of a banger but it served them well and boy when they needed to shift they shifted. And the car was only part of the story. No Mikey had a job as a bodyguard. And had done offensive and defensive driving techniques. He also knew how to disassemble a small bomb. He had been in the protection game long enough to know how to judge situations when there isn't a lot of time. And panic, he never did. But the drugs game, well it was fraught with danger. And he lived off the buzz constantly. And Boz was a good leader, no fear and no time for anyone who felt fear. No, you just had to admire the man. He was smiling and when he smiled you knew something was wrong. When he started to say things like too mad, the trouble was near. He didn't have anything to prove or anything to gain. No, people knew him on sight. And knew to leave well enough alone.

*

Biscuit carried on making love to Suzzanne and took a couple of lines of cocaine as he finished. He smiled and got up after the orgasm, the rush mixing nicely with the dope they had smoked. He smiled and sat on the edge of the Kingsize bed.

"You know something sweetness," He said and waited for his woman to open her eyes.

"Yes honey," She replied.

"I've been doing a lot of thinking, about you and us".

She smiled a returned "Careful Biscuit you may hurt yourself".

He laughed and said, "Would you marry a guy like me?"

She lit up a cigarette and looked stunned.

"Well would you?" He asked again.

She smiled "Your teasing me san'".

He got serious, "I love you lass," came the statement.

She smiled and started to skin up, "Well, would you?" Came his question again.

She smiled and finished the cannabis crumble. "We need to slow down hun".

He smiled and said, "I mean a proper wedding traditional. All the trimmings, Liam can be my best man".

She smiled and bit the wick and lit the spliff, "We'll see sweety we'll see".

He took the joint from her hand and started to puff away. He was glad he saved a couple of joints worth on his dope tray.

December first

They were all wasted and sleeping off their stone, Liam woke first at about nine thirty and went and had a piss. He then began to make breakfast. It was just a couple of bacon and egg rolls each and he didn't mind cooking. Giz splashed some Daddies red sauce on his bacon and egg roll. Then Shimmey gave his, a dash of brown. Pinkie wolfed his down without any sauce and the bacon was just right, crispy with an egg on top, he burst the yoke then ate the roll. Liam stood in the kitchen and ate his with one brown one red. (He had two). That was quite right for the dealer and owner of the hoose to have extras. It was a day away from the silly season where people made gestures of love and party, party, party was the constant mood during the Christmas period. He would visit Gemma this afternoon. Then he would prepare the money for the drug drop. This was gonna last a while he thought to himself and the thought brought a huge grin to his face. He sent the lads packing and got ready by phoning a taxi, to take him to Gemma's. He smoked a fag and drunk some beer whilst waiting for the Jo Baxi. The taxi let out a horn blast. And Liam headed down the stairwell to the car park.

He got dropped off at the foot of her terraced house just before the west end of Edinburgh. He paid the driver of the taxi and gave him a good tip, knowing that they really don't make much money, and well, well, it was nice to be nice. He arrived at her door and she smiled and let him in. If there was one constant in his life, well that was Gemma. And passionately in love with her he was. Anyway they had come away away's from being spotty teenagers to being lovers and I mean LOVERS. He was going to stay the night with her. She had no qualms about it and he was ever faithful, except you know ahemm (Katey). But that was just the once and he didn't plan on doing it again anytime soon, but women were a mystery to him. (Him and the rest of the male species).

He settled down and asked her to go and get the crack bubble so they could rock back and relax They stuck on some Muse and enjoyed the buzz. They began to talk when he told her about the score tomorrow. She smiled stubbed out her fag and removed her bathrobe. He fell straight to her pussy and began to eat, he was no novice at cunnilingus and she loved every second of drenching him in sweat and sweet pussy juices. He lapped it up and she after she had had multiples and gushed and became hard. She went down on his juicy fat cock. They then did some more petting and finished it off with spooning, I mean she knew how to spoon. His balls, his cock and even his backside. Which she thought was a major attraction point on him. His Bum.

He loved every second he was with Gemma. And he knew he would be mad to lose her. Biscuit rang the phone to Liam in Gemma's house knowing that he was there.

Gemma answered and said, "Gemma here who's holding?"

Biscuit laughed and replied, "Me doll how you need tick?" She smiled and went and got Liam. Liam took the phone knowing who it was, "Biscuit my man how yea dain?" He smiled and they began to talk, Liam came off the phone after about an hour of spraffing to his compadre. Biscuit told him that he practically proposed to Suzzanne.

Liam laughed and replied, "And are yae, are yae gonna marry her?"

Biscuit was none plus in the answer. In fact he avoided the question. So Liam let it drop. And they hung up on each other. Gemma smiled and asked, "What was that about?" Liam smirked and replied, "He proposed to Suzzanne" She laughed "About time tae," She said then went and started to roll a joint.

*

Legs, Squeak, bats and Acheo were walking back to Davy Livingstones. When a dark blue Ford Focus turned the corner and it was Boz. He had decided to play a game of hunt the cunt. Him and two other cars that had just appeared at the rear of them.

Squeak spat, "That lanky bastardin skinhead";

He then produced a dog chain. Whilst legs and the rest produced blades. "You're bloody game coming into the YBC's turf. And try and intimidate us," Said Legs, The three cars emptied and they began to run at the four of them. Squeak kept his two at bay by whipping out the chain. The rest of them were scrapping and scrapping well. They lunged at Boz and the other three keeping themselves going as perpetual motion was and an only option. They just had to stop themselves from getting boxed in. And they sliced and cudgelled their way into Broomie. They knew they could turn this fight on its heels and use their turf as an advantage. They knew how to really outsmart Boz. They just had to fight until they got to Davy Livingstones bit. But Boz twigged and went and told the rest of his foot soldiers to retreat. "This is just a wake-up call tae the YBC. Your number is up".

He then slammed his car door shut and drove away. Squeak rasped for breath as did the other three.

"This isnea over lads," said Bats "Someone tell Biscuit we're at war with the Skulls" Squeak spat again. "Aye I'll dae it". He then wandered off to the high flats in Sighthill his chain put away. Safe but easily accessible. He went and told Biscuit what had just happened. And scored himself a couple of Ecstasy at the same time. Bats and Legs and Acheo wandered the rest of the way to Davy Livingstones. Whom they had heard was holding a large quantity of dope. Soft, black, red seal beautiful gear it was part opium and very, very nice to smoke. They got there looking a bit worse-for-ware. And short of Squeak. Davy let them in and they sat down caught their breaths and began to score.

"Grandad is out in a couple of weeks," came the statement from Davy. Bats took a pull on his beer and smoked his joint. And replied, "Oh we'll need him".

Davy smiled and threw an eighth at Acheo "Why what happened?" Davy asked as Acheo produced the fifteen pounds.

"Oh we are at war wae the Skulls," came the response from Bats.

Davy smiled and said, "Your shitting me?"

Acheo began to build a cone, "No, no he's no shitting you," Came Acheos voice as he carried on putting the skins together.

"Where's Squeak?" He asked as the rest of them started to build joints.

"He's away telling Biscuit the score". Davy snarled and replied, "Fucking Skulls huh".

The rest of them nodded in unison. "Yeah". They said.

Then carried on their dope session. Squeak arrived about an hour later ee'ing out his nut, The ecstasy were good ones, They were Hearts and potent fucker's at that. He smiled a wide stoned grin and went through to the Living room. "Biscuit now knows" He said.

Acheo grinned and said, "Aye it'll no take long until we play a wee game of hunt the cunt".

*

Biscuit smiled, 'War' he thought. 'Good money to be made during a war,' he continued. 'I'll put a line on and everything'.

He had a certain reservation and that was cause of the last war he had ended up in the hospital. This time he would be more cautious. His dog Satan was a rottweiler with a vicious personality.

"Here Satan" He said as the dug went by. Satan went straight to him. Biscuit petted the Dug and it enjoyed it. As getting attention was one of the things that the dug found satisfying.

"You're a good boy Satan, yes you are, a good boy". He gave him a dog treat and scratched his ear. This some people would say ruined the dug's fighting spirit but no not Satan he was a great guard dug and had a keen sense of fighting spirit. He had battled with Police dogs and everything. And had come away the better of the lot. Suzzanne wandered through to the kitchen and made a couple mugs of coffee. Biscuit sipped his and enjoyed the aromatic Kenco coffee.

"So darling. When do we tie the knot?"

She smiled and drank some coffee, then replied, "It's a big commitment, we'll see how the land lies in a year or two".

Biscuit sighed and shook his head. "One minute all go the next..."

Liam came hame from another spectacular night of sex and drugs. Tomorrow he would meet Shaz at the train station and pick up another five ounce of Peruvian Gold Flake. One of the best types of cocaine you could get. He sat down and counted out a grand for the five ounces of cocaine. The rest would be needed for fags and drink. He smiled then stretched over picked up the crack bubble loaded it and whoosh straight to cocaine heaven. He then began to pen his diary, he had been lax lately at his penmanship. And had a lot to say. He finished by penning a couple of really stoned poems. He was no Jim Morrison but he tried. And he always had the discipline of a cocaine dealer. It wasn't a fame and fortune thing, it was an artist thing, it kept him sane.

He would write pages and pages of romantic poetry and the dark and fantastical world of cocaine. But nobody was really buying into the balancing act he had to do. And he was, well fuck it, he was growing weary of being only a second rate Poet. But all his friends showed great enthusiasms when he got the courage up to show Pinkie, Shimmey, Gizmo and Biscuit the results of his hard earned pleasure. I know I know you think it's easy to write a few lines of rhyme. Well, it's not. It was a discipline and a hard one at that. It took ages reading his stuff and believing his stuff. It was a challenge in itself. And like every challenge you had to conquer it to make it real. Liam was still a novice.

He even believed the fact that he may always be a novice, in the learning way of things. You know constantly challenging his wits and mind.

"Learn something new every day," he said and carried on writing. He reloaded the Bubble a few more times then decided he was hungry. He went and cooked himself a plate of chips and sausages. For tea. He smiled and tucked in to it, about twenty minutes after eating Pinkie arrived at his door.

"Awright Liam?" Came the question from Pinkie.

Liam smiled and let him in. "We're at war by the way." Said Pinkie.

Liam responded, "why doesn't that surprise me".

Pinkie snorted a short laugh. "Well it's us versus the skulls".

Liam sighed and replied, "When did this start? and who started it?"

Pinkie took a line of ching off the mirror and answered, "Yesterday, they tried to ambush Squeak and Legs. But you know how slippy Squeak is, they broke off their attack as they got further into Broomie".

Liam whispered to himself "Jesus".

Pinkie produced a fag and lit it then headed for the kitchen. "Got any Beer?"

He opened the fridge and fished out a Miller Ice.

"Aye man, help yourself," said Liam.

He popped the cap and went and sat and began to drain the cold frosty.

Liam smiled, "Let me guess Boz and Mikey?" He, said.

"Yes man," replied Pinkie.

"Grandad's out in four weeks," said Liam, "You know he'll have a lot to say about this".

He walked over to his technic's HiFi and put on Blind Melon Nico the first track Pusher. He loved Grunge and felt a real kinship to them in particular. Pinkie smiled and carried on racking up lines on the mirror, Liam bobbed over the mirror and took two lines quick as you could blink. He smiled lifted his head and went and got himself a beer. Pinkie looked over Liams journal and smiled, "still keeping the discipline?"

Liam walked over to the Journal just as Pinkie was opening it. He put his hand on it to stop Pinkie from reading it. "Aww come on man I love your Poetry".

Liam picked up the journal and took it through to his room. Pinkie shrugged and said, "Whatever man, whatever".

They waited in for Shimmey to appear. This was a good couple of hours whilst Shimmey scored some dope and E's. He did so from Janice Thompson, She was a stone cold fox. Not just in demeanour but in her looks, her everything. She kept her regulars happy and was always partying. She had just finished chopping a nice bit of soap bar. It was a clean smoke with a little left for herself, well when I say a little I mean about an ounce for personal use. Shimmey smiled the E's were Mitsubishis and were no bad. He got ten for sixty quid. He headed straight for Liams house. Knowing that they would be toking and snorting Ching.

He rapped on the door and Liam walked down the hall. "Who is it?" asked Liam. Shimmey smirked, "It's me John".

Liam took the snib off the door, "Awright Shimbo?"

Shimmey smiled and went straight to the kitchen and got himself a beer. "Anyone want an Eckie?"

Pinkie laughed and said, "Aye Shimmey I'll haw one". Shimmey popped his cap and sank a good bit of the bottle. He then sat next to the mirror and put out three E's. Pinkie immediately chopped his and snorted it in two long snorts. Liam did the same. The ecstasy mixing in the brain with the beer and the cocaine giving off a mellow Buzz. Liam smiled at the two of them and said, "What would I do without you two?"

They both laughed, "probably get a dead end job and live a boring non-existence life".

Liam nodded as Pinkie made the statement. "Absolutely Bang on Pinkie, i mean what the fuck do I have to do in a nine to five boring piss smelling job. Even if I can make enough money to sustain a healthy hard core coke habit. Who wants to get up at six to work till eight with nothing, barely a life, and you know the two don't mix".

Shimmey finished his frosty and said as he went to get another one, "Bang on Liam".

Liam sighed at how exhilarating his life was. "Anyway Pinkie where the Hell is Giz?" asked Liam.

Pinkie let out a small laugh, "He's scoring for me".

"Where?" asked Liam. Pinkie drank some more and answered. "I dinea Ken. He's a bit of a mystery these days. I think he's got a woman".

Liam laughed, "that's all we need a loved up Gizmo".

*

Gizmo had arrived not ten minutes after Shimmey had left. He walked down the hall and entered her living room. All he could think about was how terrific she smelled and how good the gear was she was punting. Yep he knew one thing she was sexy as fuck. She had it all and Giz was drawn into her parlour of opium and drugs with her ever enchanting presence. Giz smiled as she handed him ten eckies then she went for broke, "You wanna stay around maybe get between the sheets".

Giz's jaw dropped and he said, "Yeah doll, I'd love that," then he gulped on his saliva and she pointed to the bedroom.

"Well hun," she said, "top or bottom?" There was a whole Band marching in his singing, "Oh when the saints oh when the saints go marching in".

He stood there not able to move. Then she grabbed his hand and pulled him through the room. He was there for a good seven eight hours doing dope and getting his cock sucked. Giz abandoned all hope of getting to Liam's, no he was in Shangri la, the best place in the world and he was having sexual awakenings. Discovering things that he had only dreamed of. Oh she was gonna be a regular thing for Giz.

*

Boz and Mikey sat back and relaxed 'Message Sent' was running through the both of their minds. They began to skin up and take pills to bring themselves down from the adrenaline rush. Mikey smiled and looked out the window. He could see the windows in the other flats decorated for Xmas. It may have been a poor part of town but still traditional in its ways especially around Christmas and New Year. Boz sat back and took a swig o' whisky. It was Grouse whisky and got him to where he was going which was a nice mellow state. He smiled as Mikey sat back down.

"Everything clear out there?" asked Boz.

Mikey smiled. He had cottoned onto several snitches that were using windows and window boxes to send messages. He was, what do you call it, yeah in the know. He had already cottoned on to two houses signalling. He laughed as he caught one of them spying on the house with a pair of binoculars. He smiled as he saw this and told Boz as soon as he got back up-stairs.

Boz laughed, "did you recognise the guy?"

Mikey snorted a laugh and said, "Nah man, never seen him in my puff".

Boz smiled, "They still have got fuck all on me!" Boz started to blaze away on a doobie. "So what do we do Mikey?"

Mikey nodded his head in amazement, "There's fuck all we can dae, we can set up a couple of the enemy's locations then see how well and on the ball they are". Boz laughed and began to start on a tooter for the Smack that he had scored earlier.

*

Liam got up to have a piss. And went and got himself a coffee. Pinkie and Shimmey were both passed out in his sitting room. He smiled knowing that he had to pick up the product today. This was going to be a great end to the year. Another five ounce of snow. It was just what the doctor ordered. He would meet up with her as soon as he could, her train would be arriving mid-afternoon and he would be there. He smiled and told the other two, "Up you nae use lay aboots". Shimmey was first to wake up one eye open. "What's happening Liam?" He asked. Liam gave Pinkie a wee kick and said, "Up Pinkie up".

Pinkie whined a little and responded, "Aww come on man gies another half an hour".

Liam gave a small growl and responded, "Naw man get up I got things on the day. He suddenly realised what day it was and responded with immediate action, "Och aye its product day".

He was genuinely excited knowing that this was primo gear, best of the best. He smiled and got himself a fag.

"You need us wae yie?" asked Pinkie.

Liam snorted as if the question was redundant. "Na man I'll go myself".

Pinkie sighed and replied, "What a jip".

Liam carried on, "This lassie, well she is cautious to say the least".

Pinkie smiled and took a comfort drag and sat back on the sofa. "Aye I get it Liam".

He then went and got himself some apple juice to stave off the thirst that he had. Shimmey smiled and remembered how well him and Pinkie were being treated by Liam. But when everything was going good well, it was a sure thing that something bad was around the corner. And after all they were at war with the Skulls. One of the hardest crew's in that part of Edinburgh. But Liam was quietly confident knowing that the YBC were a solid footing in the scrapping terms, but it was all the other shit that came with the act of war, corruption and bent police.

Liam smiled and shook his head at the thought. He would just have to be cautious with his coming and goings. He would only deal with punters he knew and only the ones he knew well got in for a smoke. Just as he thought that, Giz rapped the door. Liam smiled knowing Giz's knock.

"Awright Giz my man?" came the question from Liam.

Giz who was wearing a stoned, loved up grin, smiled and replied, "Aye man I'm sound".

Pinkie was first to ask, "Where were you last night?"

Giz smiling sat down and began to skin up. "I was at Janices last night".

Shimmey smiled and then began to skin up as-well. "I bet you were".

Gizmo carried on skinning up.

"You get your brains fucked out?" asked Shimmey as he licked the Rizla. Gizmo smiled again a dopey loved up smile and replied, "Lots of blow jobs".

Liam snorted a laugh, "oh I bet you did".

Gizmo sparked his joint up and sighed. "She's fucking gorgeous. And we were hot and heavy for the next five six hours".

Liam grinned at this. "You know you can invite her round here anytime".

Gizmo sighed totally loved up and replied, "We'll see, we'll see".

He carried on smoking the joint. Shimmey smiled and gave his a little shake to tighten up the spliff. He then lit the thing. A nice bit of soap bar was what he was smoking and it wasn't to strong but not as weak as it could have been. No it had a nice opium like smell, sweet and well, well worth every penny. Pinkie took the joint off of Giz. Then toked it until it was near the roach. Giz didn't mind, so goofily he began to roll another. Pinkie smiled looked at the lit end of the joint and gave it a wee smell. 'Dark rocky' he thought to himself. Yep it was about that time of year. When dealers freshened the pot with their favourite dope. And dark rocky was like the best mellow smoke you could get. And it was usually in abundance at Christmas. Shimmey handed his joint to Liam, Liam smiled and took a whole load of tokes from the joint. He also nearly roached the Joint.

"Right lads". He said then clapped his hands. "Ive got business to deal with so you lot stay here I'll be back just before nighttime" He then left to go to Gemma's where he would count out the readies and have a quickie with Gemma. He smiled as he looked up at the ceiling. The sex was always good. He sat up reached over to his Peppe jeans and began to count out the monies for the five ounce of cocaine, seven hundred he counted out then lit a fag and smiled. Gemma smiled back at him they were in cocaine heaven. He lit up a bubble and him and Gemma rocketed to the nearest heaven. It was always nice when he got together with his lover. He would leave and ounce with her. Just in case. But first things were going to have to go smoothly with the buy.

He started to walk along to the Waverly Station where he would meet up with Shazza. He went to the platform that her train was arriving at, platform ten. He waited as the train was slightly late, due to weather restrictions. He smiled and sat down on the bench and well, well waited fir an extra ten fifteen minutes, he was excited but too stoned to let it show, the train arrived and Liam smiled as he saw her disembark from the intercity one-two-five. She approached him dragging behind her a small suitcase on wheels. Liam smiled and took her luggage. Then they both got into a taxi and headed back to Gemmas, where they would seal the deal and then she would head back on the first train in the morning. This was so as not to arouse any suspicions with the local police. As the station was closely watched with CCTV. Liam headed back to his flat and opened the door where he could hear the cheer that was going on with his three best friends. He smiled and shut the door.

"Awright lads?" He said as he walked down the hall.

"Liam!" Came the chorus of the three of them. Liam smiled and produced the four ounce that he had left. He instantly went and started to cook and cut the product. This didn't take too long and Liam held back a half ounce for him and his compadre's. They instantly got the bubbles out and began load with ash. They began to rock back the cocaine. It was good shit and left them feeling complete in the way of narcotics, they all smiled and joked around whilst the cocaine got cut with Bicarbonate of soda. This didn't get noticed too much as they were smashing a nice lump of rock. Liam knew that this was the closest to heaven he could get.

December Fifth

Liam and the rest of his crew were buzzing about getting ready knowing that Grandad was getting out the YO and it would be party, party, party. Two more weeks and his sentence ended. And they would have one hell of a good time. Grandad had become a living legend in the area. People got buzzed just talking about the antics of Grandad, his best friends smiled whilst the bubbles passed round and they spoke about Grandad. It was safe to assume he was a legend. A person of Interest. And not someone to be taken lightly. Pinkie and him had settled their differences a long time ago. Giz had dragged Grandad off of Pinkie. They had come to blows and Grandad was not going to take it. They had started to shout at each other over the price of an Eckie. Grandad was demanding his money back fae Pinkie. But Pinkie was adamant and not willing to part with the money. So it ended up the two of them trading blows. Giz had to split them Shimmey just stood and watched until Giz shouted at him. "Handers cunt?"

Shimmey smiled and said, "Na man this has been brewing for a couple of days now". Giz growled at him and decided it was best for him to intervene as the two of them would kill each other. Pinkie was not willing to take a back seat and grandad fed up taking one. They stopped after a while and nursed themselves back to a nice little stone. They shook hands then got on with their session. Liam smiled as he loved the two of them dearly and was sure as fuck not taking sides. Anyway two more weeks and Grandad would be getting out. He smiled and carried on piping his crack. Pinkie who was totally wasted put on a CD. It was *Skull Ring* by Iggy Pop. The song that came on first was. 'Frying up that hair in that little electric chair' The CD piped through the house and they had a nice buzz going. Liam smiled and said. "Right lads I got to go and visit my Auntie".

They all went, "Ah man you're killing the buzz".

He then put on his Barbour wax coat and headed off out into the miserable pouring rain. "I'll call the girls, when I'm at my Aunties"

Pinkie who had just racked up a couple of lines of ching, Smiled and said, "You do what you've got to do".

Liam closed the door and left. The cocaine was bang on and they had customers coming through their ears. Pinkie stepped up and took the reins of the product. Nobody harassed them and nobody tried to take advantage. As Shimmey was a force to be reckoned with. He was fond of showing the customers his Rambo combat knife. Liam was about an hour and just as he got back to the den the girls arrived.

"Awright Liam?" Came the voice of Shirley.

Liam smiled and opened the flat door. The four girls including Hazel, Shirley and Yvonne and Lisa. Giz arrived about five minutes after they arrived.

"Awright girls," he said, but he knew, he wasn't up to too much partying, as he had just been up at Janices. Where he had scored a couple of ounces of slate and a bag of speed. He also got his dick sucked. This was becoming a regular thing with Gizmo. Not that he fucking minded. She was gorgeous. And Gizmo loved the sexual escapades. He was going to try and take her out some time. Clubbing, hopefully with Liam and Gemma. As they really knew how to step out. Giz would raise the subject some time tonight.

Grandad fell into a narcotic sleep with the Beastie Boys, Paul's Boutique playing on his little beat box. He woke early the next morning with the drugs showing him little favour other than a good night's rest. He smiled as he went to the dining room and had his cereal and tea. He was dying for a descent cup of Baby Tea brewed by his mother. He was full of indulgent thoughts about getting out. A gramme of cocaine, and a descent bag of Kit. The kit in the jail was okay, but had been stepped on too much, it was just a lullaby to him and that it wasn't as easy, as you think to get a bag of kit in the YO. He knew he was blessed as he had gotten a couple of bags a week. This had cost him dearly but he had gotten just the right amount to keep him going. This was okay as he knew they were running a needle exchange in the YO. This had come as a breath of fresh air to Grandad. As he knew that he was a sure thing for a dirty hit. As needles were also like gold dust in the YO. But he had landed lucky as Jimmy Gandhi had been a real resource of things including music and drugs.

He was welcoming a parcel from his mother. Bars of chocolate and Tobacco. He also got some coin and a little bottle of juice. This all had to be negotiated with the screws. Who surprisingly were treating him decently. The food had a little to be desired and he was lifting weights in the rec room. He had no beefs with anyone.

And received letters and visits from his friends and family. He smiled as he counted thirteen days until his release.

*

Biscuit was snoozing silently in his den. Suzzanne was doing the house work, dishes and hoovering. Biscuit had taken a nice sleepy hit of smack. And it was coursing through his body giving him a nice sleepy rush. He enjoyed his bag of kit and was loyal to the foil. Suzzanne lifted his legs, that were on the coffee table and hoovered under them

"Cheers doll" He whispered, Suzzanne smiled and carried on tidying up. Biscuit had done some real personal growth since the war with Leeds. But war was on the horizon again and this time it would be furious and bloody. As the Skulls were a force to be reckoned with and wouldn't make it easy on them. Biscuit growled slightly in his stone.

Satan his rottweiler barked as the door was chapped. It was Shimmey and Giz, Biscuit gave himself a shake and answered the door.

"Awright Lads?" came the question from Biscuit.

Shimmey smiled and produced a bag of speed. "Are we having a session or what?"

Biscuit smiled and showed them into his den. They sat down and began to rack up lines of amphetamine.

"Perfect," said Biscuit and he snorted two lines. Shimmey racked up two more for him and Giz. They then produced skins and began to skin up. Shimmey made a nice cone whilst Gizmo made a nice wee three skinner. They toked and joked about things in the past. Scores and whores. Suzzanne sat down and began to roll herself a joint. The dope was slate and there was a tonne of it on the street, there was so much that people were getting sick of the stuff, I mean it was a nice smooth hit but it got a bit sickly the same stuff all the time. But these things were sent to try you. Biscuit smiled as Suzzanne handed him a joint. The speed was a good piece of sulph, It had come from down south and took you to were you wanted to be and that was fleeing with healthy rushes.

They tanned a good ounce of the speed. Then started to crack into Coors lager. Biscuit smiled as they were leaving, "Watch your backs lads those Skulls will try and get behind you and stick the knife in".

Shimmey smiled and produced his blade, a Rambo combat knife. "I'm easy," he said, "I'll take at least two wae me".

Gizmo smiled and shuffled his feet. "I'm easy," he said, "I'll scrap like fuck". They then headed off into the night.

*

Boz had finished for the night, he had walked his dug and was coming home from the cold wet miserable weather. He was stoned and tired and just wanted to gouch. Get some munchies then sleep. He smiled at his dug who yawned and stretched and went and fell asleep. Boz smiled at his dug, it was his pride and Joy. Boz rolled himself a fat bomber of a joint. He smiled looked at the lit bit of the spliff and said, "Fucking Slate". It was all there was on the street. But it got you to where you wanted to go. And you couldn't grumble at the fact that you only got what you put back into the scene.

Boz sat back and let the stone wash over him, it was pleasant and just what the doctor ordered. He smiled and looked at his dug. "Boscoe"

The dug immediately opened its eyes and walked with its tail wagging to Boz. Boz smiled and said, "If only you could talk huh Boscoe, yes you're a good boy". He then petted the dug and said, "Lie down Boscoe".

Boscoe did what he was told and went a lay down. Boz stuck the telly on and watched a show about, 'When Ecstasy went wrong.' It was challenging the highs and lows of MDMA. And linking the drug to several suicides. He watched it with mild amusement, knowing that in his own experience the drug was aces, and that you needed to come down properly to feel the full potency of the drug. And the best way to do that was a handful of Valium or other downer and to sleep the things off. Anyway he was laughing as the young girl explained how she had ended up a manic depressive because the stuff was to strong. On the other hand there were the deaths on the stuff, people having massive headaches then slipping into coma's and dying. It was a strange time for E's. They were either a hit or a miss.

The programme finished and Boz was smiling at the end a sombre smile that he always had at the end of a programme which told of the hardships of narcotics. He lit another Joint then went to his bed. Knowing that he had a hard day tomorrow. He had to check out the tick list situation. Some people were humming and hawing about certain drugs being too weak and they were getting nothing out of the narcotics. Boz wasn't the best person to try and hold over a barrel. But he knew soon as he showed face people would fall into line. And Mikey well Mikey was a psycho and you just didn't mess with him he would seal your fucking fate.

*

Pinkie smiled and headed home to his house in Sighthill. His mum started to read him the riot act as soon as he got through the door. Both barrels bang, bang.

"Where have you been where is your little brother...." Blah, blah, blah. He was to stone to have an argument with her so he slipped into his room after about five minutes of the punishment. He hadn't been so riled since Grandad had been on the scene. And then he took it tight from his mother as she hated the young punk. Saw nothing good in him, she was right tae. Grandad was a malcontent, a piece of dirt and would only cause trouble for James and Gary. But when he got huckled she breathed a sigh of relief. She practically threw a party. It was just a shame that Giz had gotten pinched as well. Shimmey tae. She was a bit perplexed when Gizmo had gotten a lie down, but she would see him okay. They got their heeds doon and did their time.

After he finished his custodial, Giz that was, he hit the drugs and I mean hit them hard. He was a complete addict, and his habit had really taken hold. But he remained on an even keel with it. Selling the majority of his stash. And coming up trumps. With his Viper pay, he was really pulling off the miracle and keeping up with both dealing and taking. He had been around long enough to know which way was which. Who was the most promising of punter. He kept his ear down listening to where and when the police showed up, and then avoided said areas like the plague.

Grandad was out in twelve days. And the chaos that was coming with him, well it made Giz's eyes glaze over with a passion. Pinkie smiled the closer and closer it got to his Mucker's release. The excitement made him smile in an insane way. He sat down in Ali Greys house and put on *Usual Suspect's* you know the Kevin Spacey classic. He often thought when watching this movie that Kiaser Solsei was a Broomie boy. But this was just Pipe dreams, he thought that Biscuit was a candidate for the head of a world-wide outfit. But this was like I just said pipe dreams. But in the reality Biscuit was just as connected and just as slippy, as the Kevin Spacey character. He had a tough negotiating lawyer who had got him and the rest of the YBC off with a tonne of shit. The lawyer McCrann was truly gifted in the art of challenging the Sherriff and proving that his clientele where barely involved in said crimes. He then would put forth his plea. And surprisingly it was not guilty, the majority of the time. He had let Grandad down but it was hard to help him with the Sherriff who had a huge hard on for Grandad, and Shimmey didn't help matters chanting out the YBC chant.

McCrann smiled as Grandad got his sentencing it was a powerful play by the Sherriff but it could have been worse. If the Sherriff wanted, he could have sentenced Grandad for a lot longer. But he was feeling particular generous, that showed in the light sentence of Gizmo. Grandad thanked McCrann for keeping his sentence down he could have been doing four to five years, but McCrann had pleaded not guilty. And the

Sherriff a Richard Jordan. "Mr-Tricky." they called him in and out of the courts. He had felt a bit sympathetic to the dock that day. And Grandad, well he could have been looking at a lot longer. He gave a sigh of relief as he was suited and booted for the YO.

Anyway, the time was just about over. Grandad sat back in his cell and removed the tourniquet from his arm. Then slipped the needle out his bitch. He put on some Leonard Cohen, *'Greatest Hits'*. The song that was playing was 'Hallelujah'. Perfect. He could practically taste the free air. But first thing's first get out and get to his stash and loot. The loot was simple his cousin took it and put it away under the mattress so to speak. But the drugs he had hid just as the police huckled him he had stashed his narcotics in the drying green. One of the cupboards next to the lifts. He knew it was safe cause if it wasn't he would be looking at more time. But the Police hadn't even seen where he had stashed the narcotics. The dogs had been unable to track the drugs as it was hidden in an old bucket of bleach.

December Thirteenth

Grandad got the all clear for him to be released in the next day. It was an early release and that suited Grandad down to the ground. He got straight on the phone and called Pinkie and his mother Lorna. Leon's mother offered to pick him up but Grandad was focusing on getting right back into business. He also called his cousin and told her to meet up with Pinkie and give him about a grand in change. This would enable grandad to step out in luxury. He would meet up with Pinkie soon as he got out the gates of the YO.

Pinkie was there and waiting with Jordan and a couple of other girls. Hazel and Shirley. Grandad saw them in the back seat and they had two bubbles going and they were giggling. The smile on Grandad's face couldn't be measured. No! he was on to a sure fire turn on. He took one of the bubbles as the girl kissed him, he inhaled some of the crack. And started to push his hand into the other one's pussy. Pinkie smiled and started to drive away, He put on The Doors. 'Riders on the Storm'. It was a heavy petting session for Grandad as he got driven back to Broomie. He then went straight into Pinkies Den and the three girls got naked and Grandad fucked around until the next morning.

Pinkie headed away to his blonde bit Pauline.

"I'll see you later," said Grandad as he took a mouthful of Tit and a hand full of ass. Grandad fooled around until he was unconscious. Smoking a good two to three grammes to himself. He then reached for the phone and dialled his man, Legs.

Legs spoke "Hello".

Grandad answered back, "Awright Legs?"

Leg's broke out in a grin and replied, "Grandad your oot".

Grandad smiled and responded, "Aye man I'm oot".

Legs sank some of the Becks that he had in his hand. "I take it you'll be needing a couple of bags of Kit?"

Grandad grinned and replied, "Aye man I'll send over one of the girls".

Legs smiled, "You need tick?"

Grandad smiled, "Nah man I've got the poppy".

Legs finished his beer and belched, "Tenner a bag. How many do you want?"

Grandad put a joint to his lips and said, "Three, that okay?"

Legs said, "yes man".

Then they hung up on each other.

*

Gizmo, smiled and opened the door to their sacred den, you could smell the sex and crack as you entered the hallway. It was a night of virgins and virgins only. He walked through to the bedroom and saw Grandad lying with his cock in Hazel and his hand on Jordans pussy. He was in total heaven, it was by the grace of God that he was blessed with so much. Grandad woke as Gizmo giggled and kissed Shirley, she responded with her soft lick. Gizmo was ready to explode as the heavenly Shirley kissed him back. The sweet time as he smiled as she left his lips. Gizmo gave Grandad a small nudge with his leg.

Grandad woke with a smile. "awright Gizmo?"

Giz smiled then responded, "Aye man I'm fine".

Grandad reached over and got a fag. He clicked his Jim Morrison lighter shut after lighting up. Giz smiled and produced a bag of Kit.

Grandad smiled, "I think I'll join you in a burn".

They then made a tooter each and folded over a couple of pieces of tin foil. They each unwrapped their bags and got down to a burn.

"How's Shimmey?" asked Gramps, Giz exhaled his kit. Then stopped for a pause to the cause and said, "He's fine, you know Shimmey, still game as fuck".

Grandad laughed and said, "You know we were lucky to get the same YO."

Gizmo smiled after the Burn was finished. "You got things to sort out?"

Grandad smiled and said, "I know we are at war with the Skulls".

Gizmo stretched over to Shirley and felt her quim. He was getting his rocks off with Shirley. They two went through into the sitting room, where Gizmo had her in the stirrups her hands grabbing her lovely ankles. Whilst Gizmo rode her pink bit. He was still in the mood when he finished with Shirley. He decided to give Janice a miss that day. And told Grandad that he would meet him later up at Becksy's.

Grandad carried on his day of sin knowing he would have enough time on his hands to meet up with the rest of the YBC later that night. Pinkie was enjoying a day and night of utter bliss with his bubbly girlfriend Pauline. He arrived at her door and chapped it. She answered and let her man in who was eager to get down and dirty. He sat down and she sat next to him smiling her porcelain teeth out. He smiled and got down to it by kissing her gently. They clicked and the two of them had a good necking session. They then went to her room and began to pet each other, lightly getting harder and closer to full sexual intercourse. Pinkie was in heaven. She was a dream to him and he didn't see it any other way. So they stripped each other slowly and started to bump hips and he got hard and she got wet. He had been hoping for this to happen for a long time, I mean they were getting on strong, and had lots of light petting sessions, but today they were on fine form and had each other exactly where they wanted each other.

Pinkie smiled at the fact that he had just made love to such a beauty of a dame. He sat up and asked, "You wanna meet my main man?"

She carried on rolling a spliff. "Yeah sure gorgeous".

Pinkie smiled and switched on the Hi-Fi. He put on Bob Marley 'Easy Skanking'.

"Excuse me whilst I light my spliff," James took the joint after a minute or so of watching Pauline smoke the doobie. The music played on and James reached for the phone. He called Grandad's mum who was in the middle of doing the dishes.

"Hello Che' Gratton" Pinkie smirked as she said this as only Grandads mum would come across so posh.

"Aye Mrs Gratton, its James you know Leons pal?"

She smiled sadly as they never returned the greeting in French, she had a thing for that language. "Yes James?" She asked.

James replied, "Is Leon back yet?" She smiled again as she knew the cord had been cut years ago with her and her son. "No pal Leon's no home yet".

Pinkie cursed himself lightly, "Well could you tell him that me and my bird want to step oot wae him". James winked at Pauline as she rolled another joint.

"Aye nae bother James, I'll tell him as soon as he comes in fae celebrating his new found freedom".

Pinkie smiled as they hung up on each other. Pauline bit the wick and sparked the spliff. James took the joint and savoured its dark Moroccan taste, the stuff was priceless, he had about four ounce of it and it was going fast. The punters loved it they knew it was a change to the Slate (Lebanese) that was currently on the go. It was called dark rocky 'cause it was a blend of Moroccan hashish and soft black that was wrapped around the Moroccan hashish. The delicacy that it was, well it was small star shining in the sky of pitch back. It was the sunbeam on a rainy day. The welcome change to the norm. And Pinkie loved the fact that he was sat on a large lump of the stuff. It was a nine-bar brick and was going fast. He had only three four ounce left and he had only got it two days ago.

*

Boz sat back after pining himself with a nice bag of Kit. Letting the rush course through his veins. And give him one of the only pleasures he got from being a dealer. And that only happened once or twice a week. He had made a very conscience decision to try curb his enthusiasm with smack and that wasn't easy. The main reason for that was getting a grip on his soldiers and not showing any pity or remorse for the ones who had tried to take advantage of Boz's kind streak. And his kind streak was very small. Anyway he began to go through the numbers and divided his money into two piles, one profit the other was product. He knew if he got any richer he could buy that night club in the centre of Edinburgh. He would be in fucking happy hard core heaven. He just had a couple more drops this large to make, then he would be rolling in it.

"Patience," he said to his dog, then scratched it's ear. Mikey rapped on the door. Boz answered, "Awright Mikey, my brother from another mother".

They then locked wrists. Mikey sat down and began to produce his skins and fags for a spliff. "Is it still that slate shit?"

Mikey began to answer, "Aye man there aint nothing else this side o' the toon". Boz sighed and sat across from Mikey.

"Things are too mad," Mikey laughed,

Boz continued, "Mikey it's all going too perfectly".

Mikey pulled the Rizla from out his mouth and answered, "I know man, something always fucks up when things is this good".

Boz rubbed his skinhead haircut, "We'll just have to be patient".

They then got down to toking and smoking. Boz was still buzzed of the bag of kit that he just cooked up. He smiled and said, "I got plans for that fucking YBC", Mikey finished rolling the spliff then lit it up. "You know that Grandad is oot?"

Boz nodded his head and said, "Aye I ken, he'll be all sweetness and light and full of it, I'll wait until he comes doon".

Mikey sat back relaxed and enjoyed the smooth smoke of dope. Boz smiled and produced a gramme of speed.

"Aye and he'll no get away wae it either. He is on my to do list". Mikey handed the joint to Boz who had begun to rack up a few lines, four in total two for himself and two for Mikey. They snorted one up each nostril and let the sugar rush of the amphetamine course through their heads. It was a sweet change from smack and coke.

Boscoe piped in a bark.

Boz smiled and said, "You wanna walk my dog Mikey?"

Mikey smiled and replied, "Aye man it would be my pleasure". He then stood over the dug and put the leash on it. He then took the dug a good walk, making sur it did both pish and shit. Boz smiled and racked up another two lines. He sat there thinking what the best way would be to hit the YBC.

Then it dawned on him, "Shimmey," he said then sat back contemplating the best way to get at them.

Shimmey was a local legend, in the area but his allegiance was with the Broomie boys being as he was a mate of Grandad's. Him and Gramps had been inseparable, especially after the heist they had pulled off. Him Pinkie and Grandad, It was a million pound hit. And they had got away with it. Grandad landing in the YO had been a little inconvenient. But Gramps wouldn't roll over on his mates. No matter what they offered, and they offered him a lot of police immunity stuff like that.

Mikey came back after his walk with Boscoe and took off the dugs leash. Boz smiled and handed him the record cover with two nice fat lines of Lou Reed. He took them and sat down and got down to rolling another spliff. They were listening to Pink Floyd *The Wall*. And it was at the point of the trial the trippy part that went 'Good evening worm your honour,' Boz was a big fan of Pink Floyd well him and half of Wester Hailes. They carried on their session of speed and dope.

*

Grandad was wasted when he decided to head home to his mother's, it was cold, wet and raining and he should really show face at home, so of he trudged up the road to his mom's house. Pinkie and Giz were at home having a relaxing bottle of beer each and enjoying a spliff. Liam was selling to local punters, mainly the same people that he always sold to. He was popular maybe to popular. Shimmey was at home listening to his Walkman and having a fag. He never knew the danger he was in, someone was making notes of his comings and goings. Stalking him, it was Paki and he had just got the contract handed to him and the contract consisted of Pinkie, Grandad and Shimmey.

Paki smiled, this was going to get messy he thought, then carried on up the road to his house in Clovie. He would do Shimmey first, then the rest would fall into place. At least he hoped so. Shimmey was unaware of Paki. But it was bubbling along nicely. The whole place was in either ecstasy or pain. Depending on whose side you were on. Grandad arrived at his mam's and entered, as the door didn't get locked until about ten in the evening.

"Awright mam?" came the greeting from Gramps as he walked down the hall. His mam went straight into hugging mode. She tussled his hair and hugged him. Grandad smiled as the woman lavished the most deserving of greetings ever.

"I hope you're not planning on going back inside?" She asked then picked up the phone and dialled the Chinkies.

"Lemon chicken son?" she asked as the phone buzzed and was answered by a young Oriental girl.

"Aye Mam and a portion of salt and pepper ribs".

She then proceeded to order herself chicken and cashew nuts and fried rice. Grandad left quickly as he knew he better go and check on his stash. He got to the cubby that housed his stash, opened it and to his surprise it was still there. At least eight gramme of cocaine. And a load of E's. he dived up the stairs when the Chinese just arrived not a minute to soon as he was starving. They ate their feast and she listened as he told her about the Tombs and how difficult it was to get anything inside.

He left out his habits of course didn't want to break her tender heart. So he never mentioned his addiction or the lengths he had gone to keep on an even keel with his habit. But that was a no, no, telling her he was a smack heed. No some things a better left out. Knowing would only lead to her crying a lot, if things went sour. Anyway what she didnea know couldnea hurt her. So he never approached the question. And never let on he was a chronic substance abuser. Especially heroine and Charlie.

He usually finished the night spiking his bitch. And maybe a burn or two during the day. They ate their meal then talked for a good hour or two smoking and letting things settle, She asked about Dawn and then apologized when Grandad told her that they had finished. His mum Lorna, was really regretful about it and made all the apologises. He smiled stretched out his arms and returned "Hey can't keep a good dog down."

She smiled and stubbed out her fag, "Anyway there's always someone new and fresh. And a change is better than a rest".

She gave a small chuckle at this then tidied up the dishes Grandad put the telly on. He looked at his collection of VHS tapes and thought something funny would be a change. He put on *Bad Taste* the Peter Jackson film about human eating aliens. He remembered when Pinkie and him had first saw the film they were stoned and it was a riot of laughs. Grandad had nearly been sick when the head alien drank a bowl of sick saying after he drank it, "Aren't I lucky I got a chunky bit".

Pinkie and Grandad laughed so much. You cannea buy back those days. Even his mum liked that movie, It was a classic 'Nae wonder he came up so fast' thought Grandad as he watched the black as fuck comedy. Grandad finished his nightly ritual with a small pin with about one mill of smack. It was good shit the same people who had brought in the Angel Hair. He smiled and fell into a drug induced sleep.

*

Pinkie was smiling as he went through to his bed and Gizmo followed. They shared a room in their house but that suited the two of them just fine. James started to tell Giz about his lady and how in tune they were with each other.

Giz laughed and said, "well I got that beat I'm seeing a horny blonde drug dealer who looks like Michelle Pfeiffer. James got a sudden pang of jealousy as he knew the lassie and her family.

"She the one with the hot red-haired sister that Grandad dotes on".

Gizmo smirked, "Aye how, dae you ken her like?"

Pinkie smiled and replied, "Aye she's gorgeous, you get free drugs as well?"

Gizmo scratched his nether regions and said, "Aye I get a good discount".

Pinkie who was still trying hard not to take it personally said, "Aye your Lucky Gizmo".

"Lucky," said Gizmo. "Lucky. Luck is something for the gambling man. No this is a holly Hallelujah praise the Lord miracle".

Pinkie smiled, put out his fag and fell asleep saying just as he drifted asleep "Aye, like I said, you're lucky".

*

Grandad woke at about eleven thirty. His mam was making breakfast for him and her. He walked through with the top button on his trousers undone. "Morning Mam".

She smiled and giggled and said, "Morning Son."

She had the decorations up and the radio was playing Christmas songs.

"One week to go my cherub," She replied as the mushrooms and tomato were ladled onto his plate. Then she served up the rest. He cracked his neck letting the rush from the bubbles rise. He ate and ate well. After he finished he picked up the phone and phoned Pinkie.

"Williamson residence, who's calling?"

Grandad swore silently to himself, "Aye erm I'd like to speak James please?"

Big James went and shouted, "Hey James your criminal friend is on the phone".

Grandad laughed he was a typical father who had a bee in his bonnet about Grandad. Grandad cursed again then the phone was answered by Pinkie.

"Awright Gramps, you settling into freedom?"

Grandad smiled and replied, "Aye man aye, your dad hates me wae a passion".

Pinkie snorted a laugh, "Tell me about it I got, 'the laddies dangerous and I should ditch you', speech."

Grandad smiled and smirked. "Tell him it aint broke so don't fix it".

Pinkie laughed again, "That would go down a treat, I can tell you".

Grandad spoke for the better part of ten minutes then they made arrangements to meet at the pub Misfits on Rose Street. Grandad hung up smiling. Counted out enough poppy to see him through a couple of days, that included taxi fare. He then went and got Shimmey.

Shimmey smiled and said, "Grandad your hame, how long you been oot".

"Aboot three days noo," came the reply from Gramps.

Shimmey let him into his hoose and they went into his bedroom. It was dilapidated and rustic but not without its's charms. "You want me to loan you some calli dosh?"

Shimmey smiled and said, "Aye man that would be decent of you".

Grandad produced his wad of notes and a silver plated money clip, he counted out a grand and gave it tae him. I mean if you've got friends spoil them right. Shimmey smiled and pocketed the wad of cash.

"Thanks Pal."

"I take it your split from the Heist is gone."

Shimmey counted his blessings and replied, "Had six months back rent to pay on this shitty flat".

Grandad snorted and said, "Hard times, we're all facing them".

Shimmey smiled and changed the subject. "Anyway whats up bro?"

Grandad laughed a gut buster, "We is going to get Loaded san".

They then went and got on the bus to Princess Street. Where, Pinkie and Gizmo were sat with a jug of lager each. Grandad hit the bar straight away, "Two Jugs of Fosters, barman my man?"

The Bar keep who was reading a book about Jim Morrison, "I see you're oot".

Gramps smiled into the guys face, "Is there anybody who didn't know I was doing lager and lime?"

The bar keep smiled and replied, "Aye my wife."

He then laughed and drained the pumps. Grandad took his two jugs over, one for Shimmey and one for Himself. They started their night of revelry. Grandad carried on drinking lager until a couple of hours before closing then he lined up shots of tequila for each of them. They got the salt, lemon and lime and poured the stuff down their necks feeling the warmth of the mad Mexican drink going down their throats. They were pissed.

COCAINE POEMS PART I: POET

Grandad started to go on about how Broomie had handled the last war with Leeds. Then James mentioned the downer topic 'The Skulls'. Whom apparently were just getting warmed up on the battle stakes.

Grandad asked the question, "How are Cha and Raymie doing?"

Pinkie smiled and they headed into Lothian Road to a go-go bar called Tipplers. James answered the question as they walked the hill. "Cha' is fine but Raymie wants to square things with the Skulls".

Grandad smiled and replied, "point taken" They then sat and watched as a Moloko women, beautiful stripped naked and danced to the pumping music of Led Zepplin (Gallows Pole), being the only song that could sum up the Underworld of Edinburgh.

Grandad took one look at her and said, "I'm in Love". She was beautiful and exotic, and was a great naked dancer. James was keeping an eye on the door he had a strange feeling someone was following them. You know like an itch that can't be scratched. It just bugs and bugs you. Until it settles and you turn over and go to sleep. But no this wasn't going away, it was driving him insane. He stood outside and had a joint with Giz and Shimmey, Grandad on the other hands couldn't be dragged away he was stunned and mesmerised by the woman, she didn't have a huge muff but enough to give you a good play. Grandad waited for the other three to come back in doors. They took their time.

*

Biscuit and Liam got together at about eleven o'clock at night. They had a severe case of the giggles. They were sat there smiling and laughing, high as fuck and couldn't stop giggling. The thought that was keeping them going was the big black bugger called Betty. They had a neighbour who was a cross dresser and he was big and black and didn't pull off the look at all. He had appeared one day at Biscuits door asking for a bit of dope. Biscuit looked at him and nearly wet himself.

He said to the guy, "Your fucked up enough pal, but seeing as you are clearly insane walking about like that I'll gie you a couple of gramme for nothing".

The guy smiled and shook Biscuits hand.

"What's your name man?" asked Biscuit.

The guy smiled and went, "my name is Stanley but I liked to be called Betty".

Biscuit produced a tenner bit of dope and said, "Do you always dress like that?"

The guy who was huge said, "Most of the time".

Biscuit smiled and said as he shut the door, "Be careful man a lot of people around here don't like the weird and unusual".

The guy stood smiling a small sad smile, "Thanks anyway".

He said then trapsed off to do whatever it was that transvestites do. Which apparently was party. Anyhow Biscuit were gambling on how long before someone mugged the poor fucker.

Biscuit looked at Liam and said, "I gie him a week and he'll run screaming to another area".

Liam laughed, "Two days and they find him at the back o' his door dead wie a crossbow bolt through him".

Biscuit laughed and said, "Only fucking Edinburgh".

It was a melting pot of the sane and the Insane and a totally grey area. Biscuit racked up a couple of lines of cocaine and said, "See Grandad is oot".

Liam smiled, "Aye he hit the town yesterday wae Shimmey, Gizmo and Pinkie".

Biscuit snorted a line and felt the rush, "Aye well I hope he has a good war head on him?"

The question come statement hit Biscuit with a subtle sense of urgency. He smiled and bobbed down for another line.

"Ach you know Gramps, he is cool calm and collected." He said.

Just as they were getting bored Ali Gray appeared at Biscuits door with a whole bag full of cargo. "Awright lads?" He said as he crossed the doorway. Biscuit looked at him with a coke smile and replied, "Sit doon Ali".

Ali sat down and Liam said, "We're just discussing how long until the big black Nigger called Betty buys it".

Ali laughed and produced his skins and dope. "Aye Biscuit you said he would run oot the area screaming".

Biscuit smiled, "aye sometime in the next week".

Liam started to giggle again and Ali rolled a joint. They carried on the conversation for a couple of hours recounting various weirdos and queerdos that had come through Broomie. And it was surprisingly a lot of them. Like they were drawn to Broom Toon like magnets. Some of them had their blood spilled others didn't last two seconds. They stepped over the door and were then subject to the stoners rule. And that rule was Stoners rule. They sat the rest of the night drinking and doing coke and dope.

Ali was in his element, he smiled and said, "I hear Gramps is oot."

Liam chuckled and said, "Aye three four days noo".

Ali and Gramps had cut their teeth with one and another, both of them loving the drug trade. Meeting up watching films like *Scarface* and *The Wall*. Grandad had been in care at the time and the staff in that home were corrupt as fuck. They often got Grandad to score bits of dope for them. It was a pain in the ass but Grandad got a couple of joints worth for it. Sometimes he would score for himself at the same time. Then disappear into the concrete Jungle of Broomie. Anyway Ali was having a ball, smoking, drinking and snorting coke. The music of the hour, well it was classics that Ali mainly listened to and this one was Sweet Child of Mine, Guns and Roses. They all three of them settled into a nice mellow stone, with the alcohol just finishing them off. This is what you can expect from Broom Toon. Happy Days and happy nights. Moving gently through the neon lights. But ready always alert and knowing that anything could happen.

*

Grandad got back to the Den at about Three thirty and was starving. He had forgone the usual ET kebab. And headed straight back to his and Pinkies den. He opened the lock and went straight and put the heating on. Then into the kitchen where he made himself a couple of fried egg pieces. With tomato ketchup, he sat down and switched the telly on, the James Whale show was on, then after came the Chinese cookery show *Yan Can Cook*. What this Chinese boy could do with a razor-sharp meat cleaver was unbelievable. Grandad watched it then rolled himself a spliff. Then after having the dooberon he fell into a fucking coma. And woke around about one pm. He stretched his arms and thought 'It's good to be free' He then went to the phone and phoned up his cousin.

"Awright Sully?" Sully smiled and sparked a fag.

"Yes mate, I'm doing grand, How are you keeping, I take it your out of the Jail".

Grandad laughed "I've been out nearly a week now".

Sully smiled and blew some rings. "And you're just phoning now?"

Grandad swapped the receiver hands "I'm just making sure everything is going well on the business side."

Sully smiled a little and replied, "The last three shipments have been delivered, bang on time, everybody got paid down here."

Grandad smiled, "And the Polis?" asked Grandad.

"It's all sorted mate," came the response from Sully.

"Okay, okay just checking."

Sully sighed and said, "I heard you split up with that wee chemist lassie".

Grandad sighed, "Aye, aye we split, she met someone over in America".

Sully stubbed out his doubt. "How did you hear about that?" Sully smiled and replied, "My mam was talking to your mam".

"Anyway it's a shame she was fit as fuck."

Grandad smiled, "Look I'll phone you nearer the next delivery".

Sully smiled and hung up. Grandad really needed to go down there and visit his family. He hadn't heard hide nor hair of his dad for ages. His dad was an ex-soldier, special forces, a fucking hero, and Leon was proud of that. Had often thought it would have been a nice thing if he had joined the forces and emulated his dad. Anyway he was a crook (and a bloody good one at that).

His dad was proud of him no matter what roads he travelled. Unconditional love a thing that most families didn't have. He was also patient, hard-working and of course generous. Not that Grandad needed money, he was making enough profit in the supply and demand game. His product was class A chip. The heroine was fine and I mean fine. They had go to a chemist locally to cut the stuff, that was fine by Grandad, he wasn't wanting to make a fuss. And well it was better over with as now the Skulls were making moves on the YBC Grandad didn't rattle though, he was cool calm and collected, but in a constant zen state like Mario Sperry the undefeated Brazilian Jujitsu fighter. He had started of a street fighter and when you looked at him he was so cool he had to be on drugs.

Grandad loved the UFC and was a big fan of the Gracies, a family run Jujitsu team. They were undefeated, especially Royce Gracie. Grandad loved the whole honour thing. They had proved that even the smallest of men could defeat the largest of opponents. And the fact that sometimes they wore a Gi in the cage, well that in itself was to be admired, as the heat in Las Vegas, well it's right out in the desert. Grandad kept tabs watching Ralph Gracie. Rorion Gracie the eldest. They were fighting the likes of Tank Davidge, Kimo and a number of large burly Hells angels. And of-course Ken Shamrock. The world's most Dangerous Man. He had splendid battles trying to knock Royce Gracie of his perch. But Royce had managed to beat him.

*

Boz walked down to Calders to check a couple of things out. He had an unpaid debt and that just wusnea happening. He headed to the flat that his pusher was pushing from, Ali Gray stood at the window adjacent the Guy's house and watched as Boz strode up the stairs. Ali knew he couldn't handle Boz. But anyway this was more fun than running with a gun. Ali smiled and petted the small firearm down his dukes, "I'll get you later," he said then smiled as he could hear the commotion in the stairwell.

Boz had a hud o' the Pusher and was forcing the issue for a couple hundred pounds. He knew if he left the debt they would have all taken the Piss. And that wusnea happening either. His reputation was a major part of his life and he never left any doubt.

"If you dae this again you're deed," he said and took the money from the guy's bird. Who had to crack into her sons Christmas money. She glared at her man who was supposed to be clear cut man, but had selfishly eaten into his stash. Ali carried on watching as the Capri pulled up and Mikey opened the car door from inside. Boz got in and they wheel spun their way out of the small car park. Ali smiled and got right on the phone to Grandad.

"Gramps aye you were right he commands a tight crew"'
Gramps smiled, "Was Mikey There?"
Ali smiled again and said, "Aye he came along a couple minutes after Boz got paid". Grandad leaned out

the window and spat a grogger which was full of speed and coke.

"I'll talk to you later." He said.

Ali hung up and sauntered back to Broomie. Grandad smiled to himself as if the key lay in Boz's pushers. He couldn't start anything major and sure as fuck he wasn't going to grass. As he saw what happened to snitches. They usually got stitches. Some who had repeatedly grassed were found up in the hills, dead in shallow graves. Grandad knew that he had to play this and play this easy. Grandad decided not to risk anything just yet he would wait until after Chrimbo. He sat down and lit up a fag.

December
the Eighteenth

Biscuit smiled as he got reported to by Ali Gray. "Grandad's on it," said Ali, Biscuit threw his dog a treat, a bone biscuit.

"Satan." The dog took the treat and Biscuit said, "shows your teeth". The dog knowing clearly what the command meant snarled and showed his right side of the mouth. Liam smiled and walked out of the house and headed to his Aunt's house in Calder. Leon's Uncle David was on top form with a nice chunk of change from the robbery, he smiled and dialled his nephew.

"Awright sis?" he said as Lorna answered, "Is the pain in my back teeth still around?"

She smiled and shouted, "Leon it's Doughnut on the phone!"

Grandad stretched and woke from a gouch. "Coming Mam!" He then lifted the receiver and said, "Awright Uncle you sound or what?"

Doughnut smiled and said, "Aye you wee piece o' shit you should have come and got me when you hit the toon".

Grandad smiled and said, "You know none of us can keep up with you when you power drink"

"Anyway," continued Doughnut, "Thanks for all the business you sent my way".

Grandad smiled some more, "Just as-well you were around or I would have to do business with you enemy and quite frankly fuck that".

Doughnut laughed. "You know they still keep a cell open for you and me?"

Grandad laughed, "Aye I ken but no in this lifetime".

Doughnut smiled and watched as his bit o' stuff walked by, "anyway I'm due you a drink so when you have got a minute come doon".

Grandad hung up after saying cheerie by. His mam was putting on the telly to watch *Home Alone*, then *Die Hard* then *Harry Potter*. In that order. Grandad went through and spiked his main vein. He snapped of the tourniquet and let the smack course through him it was a cool hit and he didn't even flinch. Grandad lay down and fell asleep as the rushes took him to heaven. He dreamed again of dark abysses and cruel intentions. Of dark delights and cool, cool times. Staying in the dark Nirvana of Narcotics. He smiled in his sleep and carried on chasing the dragon in his dreams. Knowing if he kept up the bad work he would get a massive treasure trove of gold coin, gems and paper.

*

Toby was upstairs counting out his Giro and paying off Shavey one of Boz's top collectors. Shavey counted it and said, "You've made my night Toby".

Toby smiled, "Is Boz still pissed off at me?"

Shavey smiled and looked at Toby "He's coming round, just keep up the bad work".

Toby smiled as he shook hands with Shavey. He walked out and left in a stolen car. Something he liked to do now and then. He would get the money then torch the car after running the engine out of the thing. Grandad passed him as he went up to Toby's to sell some product. Toby broke into a grin when he saw Grandad. "I thought you wurnea oot until after the year?"

Grandad smiled, "Good behaviour".

They embraced like brothers and Toby smiled, "Fucking "A" Good behaviour".

Grandad walked through to the sitting room sat down and began to put the papers together for a nice joint. Toby smiled and Grandad tossed him a lump of Hashish Dark rocky that Pinkie had given him. Toby began to spliff up.

"What was Shavey wanting?" Asked Grandad.

Toby smiled and carried on rolling the spliff. "what do you think he was here for, money".

Grandad started to spliff up as-well, "that must sting close enough to Christmas". Toby laughed and said, "Yeah!"

Grandad who was feeling charitable said, "You need a bung?"

Toby nodded his head in reply.

"That needy huh?" Grandad fished in his pockets and drew out his silver plated money clip. "how much do you want?"

Toby relaxed and lit his spliff, "how much can yae spare?" Grandad smiled,

"Three fifty dae?" Grandad counted out four and said, "We'll call it four".

Toby smiled and replied, "Cheers mate".

Grandad laughed, "You know you got to get back with Jen."

Toby smiled and replied, "If it were only that easy"

Grandad sparked his Joint. And lay back and relaxed.

December Twenty-fourth

Grandad woke up and headed straight for the shower. It was nine am and the day before Christmas. He showered in his Lynx Africa shower gel, then shaved. He smiled and whistled as he went back into his room. He had a good roll of money and a good stash of drugs. He needed nothing else. Well nothing but his own walking power. He dressed in a pair of Diesel jeans and a pair of Timberland boots that his dad had gotten him, on his birthday. He parted his short hair to the right and wet the floppy curly hairdo.

Lorna his mam shouted on him to, "Come get breakfast?" He buttoned his floral shirt that was very Indie. Then went through to the kitchen where the smell of bacon and sausage greeted him, that and mushrooms, eggs and tattie scones. And of-course beans. Grandad walloped into the traditional Scottish breakfast. Savouring everything, well I mean savouring it, as much as he could for having the greatest attack of the Munchies.

"You wanna come to the Church with me?" His mam asked,

Grandad finished his plate and said, "nah Mam I've got connections to make".

COCAINE POEMS PART 1: POET

She smiled and lit up a Kensitas Club fag. "Well it's no 'til midnight anyway, so if you change your mind".

Grandad laughed.

In his primary school years it was a regular thing, but now well now he could see no point. Shimmey knocked on the door to Grandad's mam's flat. Grandad answered it promptly knowing who it was. Shimmey smiled, a big cheesy grin showing all his teeth.

"How's it going Gramps?"

Grandad smiled and took out his wee cocaine kit.

"I'm awright what about you?"

He then bobbed over the little mirror and chopped two lines of quality gold flake cocaine. He took his first then handed the little mirror to Shimmey who took his line no fuss no mess.

"What we up tae today?" Asked Shimmey. The usual we'll hang about and sell some product. Shimmey smiled. "Only the Die harder's will want some so as they can space out with their women and celebrate Christmas without kids."

Grandad nodded, "We going up town to the usual pub?"

Shimmey laughed, "nah man we got a whole tonne of cargo and enough dope and powder to keep an entire chapter of Hell's Angels going".

Grandad laughed and said, "I take it we are going down Sighthill to Pinkies den?"

Shimmey smiled and lit a fag "Aye man it's a safe bet" Grandad smiled and said, "Aye well it better no fizzle oot".

They got to Pinkies den and started the music blasting *Strange Days* the Album by The Doors, they got right in the mood and the house started to fill with Broomie boys. All skinning up and drinking beer, Thunderbirds and various other Alcoholic beverages. Davy Livingstone appeared and was selling a nice bit of dope, soft black silver Lebanese.

Grandad made a purchase almost immediately as it was a nice nine bar of dope, it was soft and snaked into little snakes that you put along the Joint. 'Moonlight Drive' came on over the Hi-Fi and everybody was near the final destination. Of being completely shit faced. The party went on until four or five in the morning. Then people had to leave as well, as it was Christmas. Grandad was asleep on the sofa with a stunning little bit o' fluff. Yvonne Modiac. She was a teenage wet dream and knew how to turn a guy on. Very sensuous and very gentle. She would push your buttons at the right time with the right amount of pressure, so as you would blow your wad before you even knew what she was doing.

The Hi Fi was playing Beastie boys *Ill Communication*, it went "Soft lick ah yeah". And Grandad was in heaven as his cock was been sucked by a beautiful blonde, Grandad was in hard core heaven. He smiled as the party began to dwindle. It was Christmas and he never had so much fun in like forever. And guess what it was going to start all over again a week later at New Year.

Grandad woke at about Ten am, put on his jacket and headed up to see his mam. Shimmey heard him leave and decided to leave it. No, his was not to challenge the ways of the mighty Grandad.

Pinkie was in the room with his lady Pauline who showed up half way through the party. She had taken a taxi and arrived promptly at two am. Pinkie was immediately turned on soon as he saw her, her voluptuous pink lips. Straight away he had gotten a hard on. She was like I said earlier, a blond bombshell of a lass.

Grandad got home and sat in the living room like a burst ball, his head was banging. He was sipping a class of Irn Bru, nursing his all to heavy hangover. His mum chuckled as he put on a set of shades to stop the light from making his head worse. Grandad started to open his presents from family and loved ones, it was the usual socks Lynx shower sets, some C.D.s, Led Zeppelin and Rollin Stones. He went through to his bed and slept the rest of the morning until the Traditional dinner was served. He was like a king his mam had pulled out all the stops, Turkey, parsnips, roast potato, Brussel sprouts, and of course gravy. Grandad tucked in and had a feast with Christmas pudding served next. And the starter was a prawn cocktail. His mam stood over a burning hot stove cooking said feast and knew the appreciation was in the fact that Leon practically licked the plate clean.

December Twenty-sixth

Shimmey smiled as he played his new tape *Beggars Banquet* by the rolling Stones. "Please to meet you, hope you guessed my name", was blasting through the headphones. "But what's puzzling you is the nature of my game"

"Umm yeah," Shimmey hadn't started off liking the Stones but that song, well that song, summed up the differences in society. He smiled and bobbed his head to the "Whoo Whoo". His mum walked into his room, "Okay John, where were you last night?"

Shimmey smiled and said "Eh" His mum just smiled and replied, "Where were you last night?"

Shimmey smiled and responded, "I was at James' I told you before I left".

She smiled turned and left. Shimmey headed upstairs to have a shower. Shimmey had little idea about what was in store for him. Paki was making ready his diabolical plan. Liam and Pinkie were in the same boat, Paki was being paid a lot of money to take out the five of them. He got a small lump sum up front and a Kilo of top grade Cannabis.

Pinkie smiled and started to rack up a couple of lines of cocaine for Liam himself and Grandad, Nobody had seen hide nor hair of Gizmo who was busy sowing his oats with Janice. It was getting serious. He was dropping by every day and it was working out for him. Grandad took his line of toot. And smiled at the cool, cool rush. They loaded up a bubble and rocked back the crack and blew their stacks. Grandad smiled and put on one of his C.D's. *Led Zeppelin Two*. He smiled and started to sing along with the Immigrants song. "We come from the land of the Ice and snow" The album played out and they got a huge buzz. The crack only fuelling their angst, taking them exactly where they wanted to go.

Pinkie smiled, "See I got tabs on this guy who has been casing a couple of mansions in the Spylaw area. They are going away in a couple of weeks".

Liam sat up and said, "Aye what kind of score we are looking at?"

Pinkie smiled, "Primo, a couple of safes with a high amount of cash as well as things like collector's coins and bonds"

Liam stroked his chin and had a deep meditative think to himself. "How much roughly?" He asked.

Pinkie smiled and started to skin up. "Not sure but it's a lot, jewellery in the most teak sense as-well".

Grandad smiled and said, "I take it it's a creep and a prowl."

Pinkie smirked, "Aye man it'll be like taking candy fae a bairn".

"Aye well keep me posted on the where and when's," said Liam.

They carried on their tooting session. Shimmey arrived at the door about an hour later.

"Awright Boys?" He asked as he entered the flat,

Grandad smiled and jeered at him, "Shimbo, my man?"

Shimmey smiled and the two of them made wrists. "Thanks for the Bung the other day," said Shimmey.

Grandad looked at him and replied, "Nae bother man". Shimmey sat down and produced his Vera's and fags, then began to skin up. He had a nice bit of dope, a piece of rocky.

They carried on all day whilst Gizmo was having a ball with Janice, he was fucking and sucking and teasing Janice. It crawled past twelve into about half five in the afternoon. He woke and said "Shit".

Janice handed him a plate of sausage and onion with toast. He walloped into it then slipped on his Levi 501's and said, "I got to go sexy".

She smiled and looked at him with her cocaine eyes. "It's okay sweetie," she said and Gizmo carried on dressing. He looked at her and said, "You're my gal, your my gal".

Then he gave her a smouldering hot kiss and left. It wasn't long until he was at the door of Liams den.

"Awright lads", he said and walked in and sat next to Shimmey. They all smiled and Giz gave them an E each. They were Mitsubishi's and nice for a good buzz. Gizmo smashed one then lined up two lines and snorted one up each nostril. The rush was intense but nothing that Giz couldn't handle. They all began to rush as they smashed and did the same as Gizmo.

Using the Mirror that they always used. They carried on until the early hours of the morning. Then they all fell into a decent gouch. During which time Giz was told about the job that they had been discussing also they were talking about the guy who would disarm the security systems that each house had. Pinkie smiled as he began to tell of the guy who was a master Technician of the electric type. Pinkie smiled as he thought of the guy, he was super smooth and only did scores with people he trusted.

*

Boz looked up at the ceiling and thought. "I'm gonna show those Broomie fuckers". He was seriously pissed off, not at the fact that YBC had crawled into the top spot of Edinburgh. But the fact that they had done it so competently. With much resolve and great skill. Made the Mancunian connection with Grandad being hold of the trade. Boz was fucking fuming. They had done what he had spent four years trying to do and he had gotten nowhere. Then this upstart had created a connection whilst in the last year of High School. He knew one thing and that was there was going to be fucking bodies. He didn't care who came at him and he was willing to fight tooth and nail with the lot of them. He began to plan something and it made him smile and calmed him down. It was the formula to a great plan, he had already hired Paki but the rest was fucking legendary.

He began to roll a joint and smoke the thing and think things over, the joint and its narcotic bliss giving him room to think. Boz would deal with them the old fashioned way and that was out deal, out steal and out feel, his way in this very old fashioned war, It was about to get really old and tired. But at the same time he would have an edge over the YBC. Grandad would come out the game later, the rest would be resolved and dealt with. The way he was thinking was classic and insane but had to be done.

Grandad headed home and so did Giz and Shimmey. Leaving Liam and Pinkie to go over the plans of the Spylaw robberies.

"I meet the boy in two days," said Pinkie, "It should go smooth enough"

Liam was getting excited at the thought of robbing those rich posh fuckers. They began to toot more coke and speed, and the conversation got faster and more manic. Then the day turned into night and Pinkie sauntered home with the biggest grin he could handle. He got home and his mum was waiting yep you guessed it both barrels.

"And what do you mean you're quitting your day job. And why haven't you applied for the policeman's job that your dad and I got for you?"

Those questions, pummelled Pinkie and he just smiled and headed to his bedroom. His mum gave up and he shouted as she shut the door to her bedroom. "I'm a fucking crook woman."

Pinkie was lucky that James had been called away to the rigs. Or he would be eating that smile upside and inside out. He fell into a nice dream. And woke the next morning with his brothers grinning face over him.

"Aye well mum is away," he said, "but she left a message for you. Either work or take the High Road".

Pinkie smiled and chortled a stiff laugh.

"She meant it Pinkie."

Pinkie smiled, "I'm oot o' here anyway".

Gizmo carried on laughing, Pinkie began to pack his best stuff. All his shaving kit including his after shave. Gizmo sat and giggled at his brother saying, "Where the fuck are yae gonna go?"

Pinkie smiled, "doon the den," he replied.

COCAINE POEMS PART 1: POET

Giz laughed again, "aye like you'll get much peace doo there".

Giz started to light a fag "Anyway," he said, "They'll be clambering up tae score fae you".

Pinkie smiled and said, "That's exactly what I need, to cut my teeth in this world". Giz gave another chuckle.

"Aye well dinea say I didnea warn you," Pinkie smiled and kept on packing. "Well I'll see you later giz?"

Giz slammed the door waving and saying, "Bye".

He then went through the room and began to spliff up. James walked away cursing to himself. "mutherfucking littleshitinoabasterding brother,"

He then trapsed his way to the Den. "I should stab your ass you little shit". Grandad came to a standstill was about to shout on Pinkie but realised he was carrying a heavy burden. So he waved and went to the door of his old house.

Gizmo answered puffing away on a joint, "Awright Gramps?" Gramps smiled and said, "Where is he awa tae?" Gizmo replied "Oh Pinkie, he's homeless, to bad to sad thought. It would be better than facing Dad"

*

Liam headed to his Aunt's house to see in there was anyone needing him. He rapped on the door and his cuz answered, "Its Liam" he shouted back into the house. His aunt came along the hallway. She had just had her nightly Valium. It was getting close to New Year and everybody was settling into a decent party mode. It was tomorrow that Pinkie met up with his contact and would seal the deal. The boy's name was Jason

Thompson. But what Pinkie didn't know was his allegiance lay else-where. Namely Boz.

Liam trapsed back hame and Shimmey had been in the middle of a deal with Paki, when everything went tits up. Paki gave the nod and three other boys joined him. They hacked into him and threw him in the boot of an old Sierrea.

Pinkie was also surrounded by Boz and the rest of them. Mikey, Wayne and a guy called Scott. Whilst this was happening Liam was asleep and never noticed the hosepipe snaking into the room. Where they gassed him gently like a Jew. He woke just as Pinkie ambled into Liam's who took it as just another Hang over. Then looked closely at Pinkie whose face was just a massive red pudding.

"They told me to tell you that in the cupboard was the remains of Shimmey".

Liam opened the cupboard and a machete and the rag that was Shimmey's best Polo shirt, it was soaked in Shimmy's blood. The sirens began to ring out in the area. 'Blade runner' thought Liam who wandered down the stairs. He heard the shrill whistle of the dealers then he was done for, nothing could save him, not police not ambulance he was fucked. James sat nursing his head. That night Grandad and Giz broke into Boz's house and clubbed his fucking prize pet's brains oot. They left a note, "If good dogs breed kissing carrion look to it sir, do you have a daughter sir." They then left knowing they were going to have to go into hiding.

The End